The *Girls' Guide* to COUNTRY

Also by Kim Adelman

The Girls' Guide to Elvis

BROADWAY BOOKS
New York

Kim Adelman

The Girls' Guide to COUNTRY

The Music, the Hunks, the Hair, the Clothes, and More!

BROADWAY

PRINTED IN THE UNITED STATES OF AMERICA

BROADWAY BOOKS and its logo, a letter B bisected on the diagonal, are trademarks of Broadway Books, a division of Random House, Inc.

Visit our website at www.broadwaybooks.com

First edition published 2003

Book Design by Mauna Eichner

Library of Congress Cataloging-in-Publication Data

Adelman, Kim, 1964–
    The girls' guide to country : the music, the hunks, the hair, the clothes, and more! / Kim Adelman.
      p. cm.
    Includes index.
    1. Country musicians—Miscellanea.   I. Title.
ML394.A35 2003
781.642—dc21   2003041820

ISBN 0-7679-1418-x

10 9 8 7 6 5 4 3 2 1

Contents

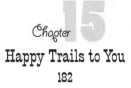

The Girls' Guide to

COUNTRY

Introduction

Y ou know that old joke "What do you get when you play a country song backward? You get your dog back, your truck back, your wife back."

Country's not like that anymore.

Turn your radio dial to a country station. It won't be hard to find because country remains the dominant radio format (on 21 percent of U.S. stations, with second-place talk radio on a mere 11 percent). You'll hear songs about short skirts, PMS, and bad hair days. Turn your TV to CMT, GAC, or VH1 Country and you'll see telegenic blondes chirping about mattress dancing and hunks in very tight jeans crooning about the joy of buying an engagement ring.

What happened?

Girls happened. Country used to have a predominantly male fan base that related to songs about boozing, cruising, and putting in hard time in prison. Those guys now listen to rap and rock, leaving the field wide open for a female-friendly sensibility to flourish. As a result, girls (of all ages) have flocked to country. Where the stars have personalities worth investing in. Where we like the music and can sing along. Where the songs relate to our lives. Where we reign supreme.

If Girls Ruled the World

When a female fan was given the chance on a televised concert special to ask hunky superstar Toby Keith any question she wanted, she asked if he wore boxers or briefs (answer: long-legged briefs). Don't laugh, even Nashville's biggest record labels recognize the importance of this topic. The official promotional material for Chris Cagle's debut album includes a similar query (Cagle usually goes commando).

Why are girls' questions about underwear taken seriously? Because record companies know women buy the majority of country music CDs and cassettes. Because CMT has a higher audience concentration of females age eighteen to forty-nine than most cable networks. Because country radio stations identify their target audience as females in their twenties, thirties, and forties.

Male performers try to appeal to that audience with love
songs and power ballads, but it's the female artists who really
score when they capture the current zeitgeist. Shania Twain's
Come on Over CD, released in 1997 and packed with female anthems including "Man! I Feel Like a Woman!" and "Honey, I'm
Home," quickly became the best-selling country album of all
time (34 million copies worldwide). In Shania's wake, the
Dixie Chicks and Faith Hill have also connected on a mass scale
(the first two Dixie Chicks albums combined have sold over 20
million in the United States alone). Less than a decade ago

record label executives didn't think "girl singers" could sell. Now everyone realizes it's a girls' world, after all.

⋆⋆ Creating the Ultimate Girls' Guide ⋆⋆

Not only do girls own today's country, girls will always tell you the best stuff. For example, why is singer Martina McBride so popular? Liz Beavers, president of Martina's fan club, will tell you that "Martina's music is incredibly moving for several reasons. One, she can *sing* like no one else on earth; her voice is instantly recognizable. Two, she picks terrific songs that people can

identify with. Think about 'Love's the Only House,' 'A Broken Wing,' or 'Blessed.' 'Whatever You Say' is a personal favorite of mine because it seems like everyone I know has been in that exact situation, where you either have to start communicating or risk losing the relationship."

To explore what makes today's country so great according to girls, we've lined up an array of female experts to give us insider information and helpful tips on music, fashion, and fun. Want statistics and facts about who won what award when? You won't find them in this illustrated handbook. We care more about what the Dixie Chicks wore walking down the red carpet at the Grammys than how many trophies they posed with afterward. Want details about Patsy Cline's career? We love Patsy and you'll find her mentioned several times, but this guide is primarily about today's music scene. Not too familiar with the current crop of CMT video stars? Don't worry, we'll get you up to speed right away. Pretty soon you too will want hair color like Jo Dee Messina's and a husband like Faith Hill's.

Get ready for country, girls' style.

Music

What music does Sara Watkins of the hot young bluegrass group Nickel Creek listen to? We'll find out! Come with us to the ultimate country music store, Nashville's legendary Ernest Tubb

Record Shop, where we'll ask second-generation country star Pam Tillis to make recommendations. At the end of each chapter, we'll offer up seven relevant CDs we've been spinning in our Sony Discman (we'll try to avoid repeats, but sometimes a girl just can't get enough George Strait).

Stars

Want to see Tim McGraw in a hot tub? We'll profile country's sexiest hunks, take a girls-only tour of the Country Music Hall

of Fame and Museum to discover superstar Trisha Yearwood's secret past, and deconstruct the movie *Coal Miner's Daughter* for tips on how you too can become a country star.

⋆* Fashion *⋆*

What's the secret behind Dwight Yoakam's trademark tight, tight jeans? The daughter of country music's most famous cloth-ier will tell all. We'll also learn how to evaluate vintage cowboy

shirts at a Nashville
shop patronized
by duo Brooks
& Dunn, and
have the style
guru who
introduced the
Dixie Chicks
to designer
Todd Oldham
suggest how
a girl could
put together
a similar
look at the
local mall.

· Fun *·*

For a modern-day honky-tonk experience, we'll ask the girl
bartender at Patsy Cline's old watering hole to recommend a

few drinks to get us in the mood, sign up for a private dance lesson from a hunky instructor at Nashville's notorious Wild-horse Saloon, and discover the trick to staying on those damn mechanical bulls. Out in the countryside, we'll find out exactly what makes Kenny Chesney's tractor sexy and get fishing tips from someone other than Brad "no girls allowed" Paisley. Just don't expect us to go huntin'.

Saddle up, girls, let's go country.

⋆⁺ One Last Thing... ⁺⋆

It seems like no one can talk about country without getting dragged into a debate about what is or isn't "country." Is Bruce Springsteen country if both Faith Hill and Kenny Chesney covered the Boss's songs on their best-selling country albums? Are the Dixie Chicks "pop" because they're played on VH1 and adult contemporary radio? Does removing the twangy sound of steel guitar and fiddles from a Brad Paisley song mean it's no longer country?

Who exactly gets to decide what lyric content, vocal qualities, chord structure, or instrumentation qualifies as the real deal? It might simplify things to say we define "today's country" or "contemporary country" as music created by modern-day performers who identify themselves as country artists and whose songs are played on country radio, music videos broadcast on CMT (or GAC or VH1 Country), and CDs filed in the country section of record stores. Ultimately, it's the listener who makes the decision whether something is her kind of country or not. But whether you find Tim McGraw real country or not country enough, we can all agree on one thing: He looks mighty sexy in a hot tub.

Dixie Chicks, *Home* (Wide Open/Monument/Columbia)—Inside the CD is a photo of a girl with a big "Chicks Rule" belt buckle. That's country, girls' style!

Chris Cagle, *Play It Loud* (Capitol)—Commando Cagle sings "Country by the Grace of God." His female fans say, "Hunky by the grace of God."

Shania Twain, *Come on Over* (Mercury)—Thirty-four million people worldwide came on over and liked what they heard.

Martina McBride, *Greatest Hits* (RCA)—The songs fan club president Liz Beavers mentioned, plus fifteen other winners.

Nickel Creek, *This Side* (Sugar Hill)—If you thought bluegrass was old-man music, the cuties in Nickel Creek will change your mind.

Dwight Yoakam, *Under the Covers* (Reprise)—Ever wondered what Dwight Yoakam looks like in bed? Buy this CD just for the photos of Dwight between the sheets.

Various Artists, *Totally Country* (BNA)—Can't get more country than *totally* country! A good way to sample recent big hits.

Chapter 1

Welcome to the Country Club

erhaps it began when you heard Faith Hill on the adult contemporary radio station they play at work. After humming along to her infectious "Breathe," you decide to pick up her album next time you're at Target. Listening to the CD, you find your favorite song is her "Let's Make Love" duet with husband Tim McGraw. The next day you're home watching TV. Flipping through channels you catch a glimpse of the dynamic duo performing that very song in an extremely glamorous video shot in Paris. Who knew your satellite system carried CMT!

You find yourself watching CMT every time there's nothing good on regular TV. Who's Phil Vassar? You don't know, but you like his video for "American Child," where he cavorts in wheat fields with his real-life little girl. Next time you're in Target, you buy his CD. You also snag a Jo Dee Messina album because not only do you enjoy the redhead's spunky videos, you've noted that Phil Vassar's penned her hits "I'm Alright" and "Bye Bye." Even more incentive: Tim McGraw coproduced Jo Dee's record.

Your car radio becomes permanently tuned into the country station, where they play Faith, Tim, Phil, Jo Dee, and all the CMT regulars. You hear on the radio that Phil Vassar and newcomer Carolyn Dawn Johnson will be opening for Kenny Chesney when he plays the local amphitheater. You buy tickets. At the concert, you're envious when the fan in the seat next to you mentions that the last time she saw Kenny Chesney, he was opening for Tim McGraw. She also tells you to join Phil Vassar's fan club so next time you can participate in the backstage meet-and-greet before the concert.

As you write the check to join Phil Vassar's fan club, you realize there's no going back. You've gone country for good.

A Grand Adventure

There's never been a better time to be a country fan. Not only are there scads of exciting artists making music right now, but there are over eight decades of back catalog to explore. Just as

Phil Vassar might have been your introduction to Jo Dee Messina, you'll find one artist will lead you to another. As you follow these trails, you'll delight in one discovery after another. And while it's possible to have never heard George Jones or Tammy Wynette and still consider yourself a country fan, sooner or later you'll be exposed to something that will lead you to them, or further back, to singing cowboy Roy Rogers, or even further back, to the singing brakeman, Jimmie Rodgers.

Don't worry, we won't bore you with a time line tracing how the mountain string band sound transformed and mutated into cowboy music, Western swing, bluegrass, honky-tonk, rockabilly, the Nashville sound, new traditionalism, alt-country, and twang-lite crossover. We know new converts don't encounter music in chronological order. You start somewhere and follow where your interest leads. Perhaps your enjoyment of country doesn't go as far back as the George Jones and Tammy Wynette duets right now, but in a few years it might. Then you'll be blown away by the many amazing songs waiting to be experienced.

Everyone Is Welcome

Perhaps because it's always been the music that chronicles the life of ordinary folks, you'll discover that your fellow country fans range from presidents to barflies, octogenarians to toddlers. Singer/songwriter Pam Tillis explains, "Country music is for everybody. It's not exclusive. Sort of like blue jeans. Everybody is welcome to wear a pair of blue jeans if they so desire. Whereas with certain kinds of rock, sometimes part of the fun is feeling like you're part of a special club, like you get it and nobody else does. Country music to me is just not like that. It's for everybody."

⋆₊⋆ *Country Close Up* ⋆₊⋆

That's Jodie Weckman with hotshot band Trick Pony. Jodie has had her photo taken with Phil Vassar, Jo Dee Messina, Kenny

Chesney, the Dixie Chicks, and even Shania Twain. Who is Jodie Weckman? Just a girl who likes country music. Since she's clearly got being a fan down to an art, we asked Jodie to share some tips for fans just starting on their country adventure.

To find out when artists are coming to your town, Jodie recommends checking the stars' websites for their posted tour schedule. Pollstar, Ticketmaster, and Clear Channel also have extremely helpful websites.

When it comes to scoring tickets, you can always buy them, but it's even better to win them. Jodie suggests doing all the radio station giveaway contests, especially in-store promotions where you have to put your name in a box (not many people actually make the effort, so your odds of winning are much better). Jodie's won prizes ranging from VIP seating to pre-show party passes. She even got to meet Shania Twain backstage thanks to a promotion run by her local radio station.

Join a star's fan club for preferred seating and meet-and-greet opportunities. Each artist's policy is different, but you usually get a chance to say hello to the star before the concert, pose for a picture, and get an autograph. Liz Beavers, president of Martina McBride's fan club, reports "Martina tries to arrange fan meet-and-greets at her concerts, and most everyone writes me later telling me how charming and down-to-earth she is." Jodie names Keith Urban, Rascal Flatts, Trick Pony, and Craig Morgan as up-and-coming artists who are especially friendly at their meet-and-greets.

If you don't live in an area where country stars come to perform, Jodie recommends going to Fan Fair in Nashville. This
annual four-day all-star event is a great way to meet and see
performances from practically every country star you can think
of. Surrounded by over a hundred thousand of your fellow
fans, you'll be overcome by the feeling of community. And
you'll know that everyone there is thinking the same thing:
There's nothing better than being a country fan!

Welcome to the club.

Phil Vassar, *American Child* (Arista)—Not only is this
piano man apparently a very attentive father, he's a
talented songwriter and extremely entertaining in
concert. Join his fan club ASAP.

Jo Dee Messina, *I'm Alright* (Curb)—Packed full of catchy
tunes. Even the ones Phil Vassar didn't write are fab.

George Jones and Tammy Wynette, *George & Tammy's
Greatest Hits* (Sony)—Sooner or later you'll end up in
George and Tammy's world. Start off with a collection
of their amazing duets.

Trick Pony, *On a Mission* (Warner Bros.)—They look a
little cartoonish, but so does Buck Owens! Heidi

Newfield has a powerful voice that reeks of old-fashioned honky-tonk.

Rascal Flatts, *Melt* (Lyric Street)—Girls melt when this trio of charmers take the stage. See them live to fully appreciate their charisma.

Keith Urban, *Golden Road* (Capitol)—This nice blond Aussie plays a mean guitar.

Craig Morgan, *Love It* (Broken Bow)—Fan Jodie Weckman highly recommends giving this not-so-well-known but super-nice guy a listen.

Chapter 2

Seven Essential Hunks

Let's go "Strait" to the good stuff: all the fabulous hunks in hats. Today's country is overrun by so many stone-cold sexy gents that it's almost too much of a good thing! Every time you turn on CMT there's another hottie demanding your attention. They come in twos (Brooks & Dunn), threes (Rascal Flatts), fours (Lonestar), and sixes (Diamond Rio). They're even being imported from Australia (Keith Urban) and Canada (Emerson Drive)! While all of these contenders are extremely worthy, there are seven men who define the genre. Consider them contemporary country's Top Guns.

1 George Strait

Sign: Taurus (b. May 18, 1952)

Height: 5'10"

Eyes: Green

Under the hat: Strong head of hair (Witness the "She'll Leave You with a Smile" video)

Availability: Taken (married since 1971 to high school sweetheart, Norma)

First album: *Strait Country* (1981)

Sexiest album cover: George in a bar, *Always Never the Same* (1999)

Song you've probably heard: "Amarillo by Morning"

Female fan favorite: "You Look So Good in Love"

Why he's essential: George Strait is today's quintessential male country singer. He has the career that all the "hat acts" who ape him hope to have.

Still on top of his game after two decades, George has more number-one singles (fifty, with more certain to come) than any other country artist, and his older hits are still in regular rotation on country radio. Strait's magic formula for picking hits? He listens first to a song's melody. If it grabs him, he then focuses on the lyrics.

When it comes to touring, George Strait is also the act to beat. In fact, at one time or another he's hired most of the other essential hunks to be his opening act.

George Strait has even starred in a Hollywood movie, *Pure Country,* which is basically a contemporary country take on the old Elvis movie formula: See George lovin', fightin', and singin' up a storm in glorious Technicolor! In true Elvis fashion, the sound track is better than the film.

"With George Strait, there are no negatives," points out music journalist Beverly Keel. "He's beautiful, he sings well, he's a gentleman, he's humble. He's a cowboy, lives on a ranch, been married to the same woman forever. How can you not like George Strait?"

2 Garth Brooks

Sign: Aquarius (b. February 7, 1962)

Height: 6'1"

Eyes: Blue

Under the hat: Graying and thinning (looks good cut very short)

Availability: He's divorced from his first wife, but odds are he won't remain single for long

First album: *Garth Brooks* (1989)

Sexiest album cover: Garth in a stable, *Sevens* (1997)

Song you've probably heard: "The Dance"

Female fan favorite: "If Tomorrow Never Comes"

Why he's essential: Garth Brooks is the Oprah of country music. People either love him or hate him, but no one can deny his preeminence (the Recording Industry Association of America has anointed him America's biggest-selling solo recording artist, thanks to 105 million units sold). Like Ms. Winfrey, Garth took his format to a previously inconceivable level of popularity based on an intense connection with his audience.

To appreciate what Garth brings to the table, check out Mark Chesnutt's draggy version of "Friends in Low Places" or original demos by Garth's songwriters. No one can match Brooks's drama and emotion. A writer himself, he's passionate about recognizing the genius in other songwriters' material.

The first artist to bring a stadium rock-and-roll sensibility to country concerts, Garth credits high-energy cowboy singer Chris LeDoux for teaching him how to be a wild man on stage. Back in 1990, when Garth was opening for Reba McEntire, savvy Reba watched the audiences react to Garth's antics and knew right then he was going to be unstoppable. But not even Ms. McEntire could have predicted that seven years later Garth would be playing New York's Central Park before an audience of one million, with another 14 million tuning in to watch it simulcast on HBO. (This concert and a 1992 television special are available on video.) Since Garth says he won't tour anymore (country's biggest overachiever is fond of contemplating retirement), these taped performances might be the only way to see him in action.

His two-CD live album is also a treat. When it was released in November 1998, *Double Live* set a record for first-week sales (1.08 million copies). When it became the best-selling live album ever, no one was really surprised. Just another day at the office for Garth Brooks.

Alan Jackson

Sign: Libra (b. October 17, 1958)

Height: 6'4"

Eyes: Blue

Under the hat: Receding hairline (search out his 1993 video collection *Alan Jackson Livin', Lovin' and Rockin' That Jukebox* to see him hatless backstage)

Availability: Taken (married since 1979 to hometown girl, Denise)

First album: *Here in the Real World* (1989)

Sexiest album cover: Alan in a boat, *Everything I Love* (1996)

Song you've probably heard: "Where Were You (When the World Stopped Turning)"

Female fan favorite: "Chattahoochee"

Why he's essential: A contemporary of Garth's (their first albums debuted the same year), Alan Jackson has consistently been one of country's strongest singer/songwriters (he's written twenty-one of his twenty-nine number-one hits). His heartfelt reaction to 9/11, "Where Were You (When the World Stopped Turning)," catapulted him to a whole new level.

In an era when many songs are indistinguishable and eminently forgettable, Alan Jackson's thoughtful rumination on our nation's great tragedy reminded everyone of the power of country music. But don't write Alan off as an earnest do-gooder. He's also the man who wrote a song especially for Faith Hill ("I Can't Do That Anymore") and recorded the guilty pleasure hit "It's Alright to Be a Redneck" (which he did not write). Alan's genius is that he knows country songs run the gamut from silly to sublime.

In 2002, Alan dominated the Country Music Association Awards, coming away with five trophies, including Entertainer of the Year, which he modestly accepted saying he wasn't as entertaining as other performers because his concert style is to just stand there and sing. But when it comes to music videos, Alan really shines. Who can forget him water skiing in shredded jeans for his now-classic video "Chattahoochee"? For that alone he deserves Entertainer of the Year every year!

4 Tim McGraw

Sign: Taurus (b. May 1, 1967)

Height: 6'

Eyes: Brown

Under the hat: Was thinning, but then began thickening (looks great hatless in the Paris-set "Let's Make Love" video)

Availability: Taken (married since 1996 to Faith Hill)

First album: *Tim McGraw* (1993)

Sexiest album cover: Tim in extreme close-up, *Everywhere* (1997)

Song you've probably heard: "I Like It, I Love It."

Female fan favorite: "It's Your Love" (sung with Faith Hill)

Why he's essential: Tim McGraw is the leader of the post-Garth generation, the young guns who assumed they would achieve Garth-level world domination only to be surpassed by the supernova Shania Twain and her female cohorts.

Tim has seen his wife, Faith Hill, go from being his opening act to a megastar. Instead of being bitter, he cheers Faith on and lends his singing and/or producing support to other megastars-to-be Martina McBride and Jo Dee Messina. What a guy!

Not a writer, Tim learned the importance of getting good material after his first album didn't include a single breakout hit. Like Garth, Tim's got an ear for catchy tunes and a weakness for classic rock (he's famous for a great live version of Steve Miller's "The Joker"). While he always seems a little stiff performing on televised award shows, in concert McGraw really lets loose. If you want to get a taste of what he's like in concert, just watch the video for "The Cowboy in Me." Tim's got smoldering down to an art.

5 Kenny Chesney

Sign: Aries (b. March 26, 1968)

Height: 5'6"

Eyes: Blue

Under the hat: Not much left (looks nice with remaining hair buzzed extremely short in the video for "How Forever Feels")

Availability: Up for grabs (*Country Weekly* named him "Country's Hottest Bachelor")

First album: *In My Wildest Dreams* (1993)

Sexiest album cover: Kenny in water, *Greatest Hits* (2001)

Song you've probably heard: "Young"

Female fan favorite: "How Forever Feels"

Why he's essential: Known for radio-friendly music, extremely popular videos, and concerts packed with screaming female fans of all ages, Kenny Chesney is today's prototypical star.

With his 2002 *No Shoes, No Shirt, No Problems* album, Kenny joined the select group of country stars who can sell enough albums right out of the gate to debut atop both the country and Billboard 200 charts. While some accuse the island-lifestyle-loving Kenny of being warmed-over Jimmy Buffet, he confesses to be channeling the late Conway Twitty. When choosing songs to record, he follows the Twitty mandate to sing things women want to hear. This and the fact that he's single have made him very popular with the ladies.

A good friend of Tim McGraw's, Kenny toured with Tim in 2000, before he became a headliner in his own right. There was some trouble in the parking lot at one show involving Kenny, a horse, and some cops, and the resulting scuffle got Tim and Kenny thrown behind bars and garnered a lot of press. But the most memorable event of that tour was caught on tape and in-cluded in Kenny's "Don't Happen Twice" video: sharing a stage with his buddy, the diminutive singer launched himself at Tim, wrapping his legs around McGraw's waist and holding on tight. This playful moment perfectly symbolizes Kenny's identifica-tion with his audience. Who hasn't wanted to do that?!

Toby Keith

Sign: Cancer (b. July 8, 1961)

Height: 6'4"

Eyes: Blue

Under the hat: Receding (but still happy to go hatless in many of his videos)

Availability: Taken (married since 1984 to hometown girl, Tricia)

First album: *Toby Keith* (1993)

Sexiest album cover: Toby pictured in both white and black hats, *Dream Walkin'* (1997)

Song you've probably heard: "How Do You Like Me Now?!"

Female fan favorite: "You Shouldn't Kiss Me Like This"

Why he's essential: Toby Keith's first single, "Should've Been a Cowboy," was the most played song on country radio in the 1990s. His "How Do You Like Me Now?!" will most likely dominate throughout this decade. While most songs come and go, a Toby Keith tune stays on the airwaves and in the public consciousness.

Like Tim McGraw, Toby remembers the days when a now-legendary female superstar opened for him (in his case, it was Shania Twain). Like Kenny Chesney, he subscribes to the Conway Twitty theory that men in country songs should be more romantic than they are in real life. But where Toby diverges from his peers is his songs are better known than he is. Kay Johnson, president of Toby Keith's fan club, notes that when people first see the singer in concert they "are usually surprised at the older songs—they knew and loved the music, but didn't know who sang them."

Video has helped put a face to the songs. Toby's fun, flashy, confident pieces have helped solidify his persona. Becoming a commercial spokesperson for 10–10–220, Coors, and Ford Trucks have also raised his profile. Now being offered *Reba*-like sitcoms to star in, Toby Keith is poised to be country's next big all-media entertainer.

7 Gary Allan

Sign: Sagittarius (b. December 5, 1967)

Height: 5'11"

Eyes: Blue

Under the hat: Full head of hair

Availability: Taken (married to wife number three)

First album: *Used Heart for Sale* (1996)

Sexiest album cover: Gary in a suit, *Smoke Rings in the Dark* (1999)

Song you've probably heard: "Smoke Rings in the Dark"

Female fan favorite: "The One"

Why he's essential: Gary Allan represents the newer male acts coming up in a post-Shania world. Not interested in crossover appeal, Gary and his peers vow to put some grit back into country.

Gary Allan labels most country songs on the radio today as "fluff" and says his audience consists of people "starving for something honest." A proud Californian from the Bakersfield tradition, he doesn't hark back to middle-of-the-roaders like Conway Twitty. His idols are Buck Owens and Merle Haggard. "Buck and Hag, they didn't care what anyone thought, they did their own thing," Gary says in his official record company bio. "And that's what I'm trying to do." Gary, of course, is much cuter than Buck or Hag.

George Strait, *Strait Out of the Box* (MCA)—Four CDs and it still doesn't have every hit. It does have a very nice seventy-two-page booklet with lots of hunky pictures.

Various Artists, *In the Beginning: A Songwriter's Tribute to Garth Brooks* (VFR Records)—Actively involved in this project, Garth offers remarkably candid commentary about his songwriter cronies in the twenty-two-page insert booklet.

Alan Jackson, *Under the Influence* (Arista)—Alan Jackson covers some of his personal favorites, including classics by Merle Haggard, Hank Williams Jr., Gene Watson, and Charley Pride.

Tim McGraw, *Tim McGraw and the Dancehall Doctors* (Curb)— Baseball legend Tug McGraw's kid keeps knocking 'em out of the ballpark.

Toby Keith, *Greatest Hits Vol. One* (Mercury)—You'll be surprised by how many of Toby's songs you already know, including the Sting ditty "I'm So Happy I Can't Stop Crying."

Kenny Chesney, *Me and You* (BNA)—Sure, he's short, but so's Tom Cruise! See him in concert and you'll be convinced this guy's got talent to burn.

Gary Allan, *Smoke Rings in the Dark* (MCA)—Keep your eye on Gary Allan. The surfing cowboy is destined for greatness.

everything's
gonna be
alrigh

Girls with Guitars
and Guy Trouble

One day after an inspiring session of girl talk, Deana Carter sat down with cowriter Rhonda Hart to write a lighthearted modern girl's lament. In their song, the trailer-dwelling heroine complains that when she comes home from work looking for a little romance, her man is more interested in downing a Bud and watching cable than appreciating her new shoes, hairdo, and manicure. Female country fans laughed with delighted recognition when they heard the song's title: "Did I Shave My Legs for This?" Deana's 1996 tune became a smash hit.

Although it's hard for us in the post-Shania world to believe, for decades the country music industry didn't think "girl singers" could sell records. It has taken generations of women writing and singing songs with wide appeal to prove that there is indeed a market for storytelling told from a female point of view. Listen up, Nashville, girls rule!

Hello Kitty

The pioneer who cleared the path for future female megastars was guitar-wielding, gingham-frocked Kitty Wells, the very first woman to top the country charts. Kitty's 1952 song "It Wasn't God Who Made Honky-Tonk Angels" was an "answer song" to a Hank Thompson hit called "The Wild Side of Life." Kitty's response (which she did not write) lays the blame for juke-joint adultery squarely on the shoulders of husbands who conveniently forget they are married when they go bar hopping. Many female listeners sided with Miss Wells and bought enough copies to make her manifesto number one for six weeks straight.

After Kitty's runaway success, record companies were slightly more willing to take a chance on girls with guitars and guy trouble. Enter the golden era of Patsy Cline, Loretta Lynn, and Tammy Wynette. These women sang hard-hitting stories from a woman's point of view, songs that we still cherish to this day. Patsy Cline hit the charts with "Walkin' After Midnight" in 1957 and "Crazy" (written by a young Willie Nelson) in 1961. Loretta Lynn debuted "Honky-Tonk Girl" in 1960 and followed up with great don't-mess-with-me tunes like "Your Squaw Is on the Warpath," "Fist City," and "You Ain't Woman Enough to Take My Man." But Loretta's ultimate female liberation song was a hosanna for birth control called "The Pill," which she did not write but which, like many of her too-frank-for-conservative-radio songs, caused controversy. Tammy Wynette, of course, contributed the ultimate dubious advice song "Stand By Your Man," in which women are counseled to forgive men for their transgressions. Decades later Hilary Clinton slammed the 1968 anthem and Lyle Lovett covered it without changing the words.

Hello Dolly

The next girl who came along and changed all the rules was Dolly Parton, who achieved previously undreamed of crossover success with massive country/pop hits like "Here You Come Again."

Although happily married for decades, Dolly's biggest hit was also inspired by man trouble. For years she was profession-ally partnered with singer and syndicated television star Porter Wagoner. When Dolly felt it was time to move on, Porter re-fused to accept her decision. She finally resorted to communi-cating via a song, which she wrote in one sitting. She was on such a roll she even penned a second composition that night.

Those two tunes were "I Will Always Love You" and "Jolene." After she played Porter Wagoner "his" song, she was surprised by his reaction: Porter told Dolly she had a monster hit on her hands.

And Then Came Shania

After Dolly came superstars Barbara Mandrell and Reba McEntire, showy entertainers who also appealed to an audience beyond the country fold. "But until a dozen or so years ago, the record companies weren't really convinced that women really sold," says music journalist Beverly Keel. "Shania Twain raised the roof on what can be expected sales- and career-wise. Now everyone is scrambling to find the next Shania Twain, Faith Hill, or Dixie Chicks."

But as Beverly Keel points out, the music made by today's women is a lot different from "your mother's country music. Songs no longer depict a woman being defined by her man. Lorrie Morgan is really good at capturing this in songs like 'Standing Tall.' Instead of saying take care of your man, Shania Twain says, 'Hey, I'm home from work, take care of me.' These are not male-bashing women. These are women who love men, but they love themselves more. Things have definitely changed."

Set Your Inner Shania Free

Any girl can be the next Dolly or Tammy or Shania any night of the week if she knows where to find the local karaoke bar.

Oh sure, you can always power through Dolly's "I Will Always Love You," but it's a tired choice. For the girl who wants something a little off the beaten path but still a recognizable crowd pleaser, we suggest the following Ten Great Girl Songs with Attitude. Trust us, they're surefire applause-getters.

"Walkin' After Midnight"—No fear of the dark for lovelorn Pasty Cline. Yes, it's a little too familiar, but if you add some "These Boots Are Made for Walking" moves you'll find this song is unbeatable.

"Your Good Girl's Gonna Go Bad"—Almost anything in the Tammy Wynette catalog is solid, but her second hit song is an overlooked gem. The best way to present this rollicking number is back to the audience, shaking your rump and looking suggestively over your shoulder. Add arm movements for full dramatic effect.

"Rose Garden"—Lynn Anderson wants to make one thing clear: She doesn't make promises she can't keep. This swinging 1970 tune is still a winner if you rethink it with a sassy waitress mind-set.

"Would You Lay with Me (in a Field of Stone)"—Teen queen Tanya Tucker asks how much her man is willing to endure to be with her. Think Lolita.

"Harper Valley P.T.A."—Jeannie C. Riley's classic about a kick-ass mother facing down a bunch of small-town hypocrites has to be performed in a miniskirt. Finger pointing is also mandatory.

"Fancy"—Reba McEntire powers through Bobbie Gentry's melo-dramatic mother-daughter prostitution saga. There's no reason to be subtle with this one. Give it a lot of Cher.

"Girls with Guitars"—Wynonna delivers Mary Chapin Carpen-ter's tale of girls with Jimi Hendrix dreams. Air guitar optional.

"Cleopatra, Queen of Denial"—It's the law: Pam Tillis's comedy clas-sic must be performed with "Walk Like an Egyptian" moves.

"Honey, I'm Home"—Shania Twain gets through a hellish day know-ing she has a love slave waiting at home. Play it straight and you'll alienate the guys. The trick with this one is to do it like Shirley Temple. Seriously, it's very funny sung by a Kewpie doll.

"When God-Fearin' Women Get the Blues"—Martina McBride's song suggests that the cure for the blues might be found in the shoe department at Neiman Marcus. For this one, drag up your friends for some Supremes choreography. Just make sure they understand that you're Diana Ross.

And if all else fails, pull out "I Will Always Love You." It worked for Whitney Houston, it worked for Dolly, and it will work for you. Good luck!

Deana Carter, *Deana Carter Collection* (Capitol)—What a bargain! Rather than buying Deana's first two albums you can buy this collection, which has the leg-shaving song, plus "Strawberry Wine," "We Danced Anyway," and "Count Me In."

Patsy Cline, *Heartaches* (MCA)—Patsy never disappoints.

Tammy Wynette, *Anniversary: 20 Years of Hits* (Epic)—The best marriage-song duets with George Jones ("Golden Ring," "Two-Story House") plus "D-I-V-O-R-C-E."

Various Artists, *Queens of Country* (Gnp Crescendo)— Hunt down this 1995 compilation! All a karaoke queen's favorites, with an added bonus of Jessi Colter's "I'm Not Lisa."

Sara Evans, Martina McBride, Mindy McCready, Lorrie Morgan, *Girls' Night Out* (BMG/BNA)—Four fabulous divas on one compilation CD, what more could you ask for?

Reba McEntire, *Greatest Hits Vol. Two* (MCA)—Her "Is There Life Out There" song about a mother going back to school inspired many housewives to do the same.

Pam Tillis, *Greatest Hits* (Arista)—Has Pam been reading our diary? These twelve songs could be our life story put to music.

Chapter 4

ALISON KRAUSS + UNION STATION
NEW FAVORITE

The Hottest
Trend Going

Take a look at the guy sitting next to Alison Krauss in the foreground of the *New Favorite* album cover. That's Dan Tyminski, the man who did George Clooney's singing in *O Brother, Where Art Thou?* Dan's wife said having her hubby's voice coming out of heartthrob Clooney was like a fantasy come true. A lot of people agreed, buying more copies of the bluegrass-heavy sound track than they did of Garth Brooks's latest offering. One million more, in fact.

As a result, country music took one of those unexpected turns that keeps the genre so exciting. Although bluegrass music has been around since 1939, when Bill Monroe first added a caffeinated kick to old-time string band music, it suddenly became sexy. CMT put together a Bluegrass Rules Week and scored record-breaking numbers. Over 7 million people tuned in to discover what Elvis knew back in 1956, when he, Carl Perkins, and Jerry Lee Lewis entertained themselves by imitating Bill Monroe's trademark "high, lonesome" sound and multipart vocal harmonies. Bluegrass is fun.

Blonde and Blue

Quick, who's the first blond babe you associate with bluegrass? Elly Mae Clampett, of course. *The Beverly Hillbillies* theme music was performed by bluegrass legends Lester Flatt and Earl Scruggs, who got their start as Bill Monroe's Blue Grass Boys. Flatt and Scruggs's fast-paced, intricate picking also accompanied Faye Dunaway's stylish blond gangster in the 1967 flick *Bonnie and Clyde*.

"Bluegrass gives the musicians more of an opportunity to show their skills," says fan Kori Frazier. "The genre takes basic acoustic instruments and puts them together in any number of combinations, so it is the instrumentation rather than the lyrics that really draws you in."

Although Ricky Skaggs and Vince Gill are very active in today's bluegrass scene, Alison Krauss and the guys in Union Station give it sex appeal. Alison used to be a fiddle-totting, stocky brunette famous for getting her record deal at age fourteen and winning her first Grammy at nineteen (she's won a dozen since). Now she's a blond sylph wandering around in a little slip dress singing in her stunningly angelic voice about "The Lucky One." Is it any wonder CMT puts her videos in constant rotation?

After years of being the most famous female face in bluegrass, Alison is determined to help other bluegrass-and-beyond young guns. Most recently, she's been busy producing albums by a trio calling themselves Nickel Creek.

Way Cuter Than the Blue Grass Boys

Although they've been playing together for years as a kids band on the bluegrass festival circuit, violinist Sara Watkins still can't believe how fast everything has come together for the fair-haired trio. Sara, guitarist brother Sean, and mandolinist Chris Thile have had two hit CDs, tons of airplay on CMT, and a *New York Times* profile, the headline of which read "Bluegrass That Can Twang and Be Cool Too . . ." To top it off, *Time* magazine picked them as one of five "Music Innovators for the Millennium."

What makes Nickel Creek so exciting is they blend traditional bluegrass with a young person's adventurous sensibilities. Their CD player is loaded with Elliot Smith, Radiohead, Bela Fleck, Turtle Island String Quartet, Edgar Meyer, Pat Metheny, Murray Perahia, and Bach. It all comes out in their music, which some have called "Youth Grass."

Gold in Them There Hills

Another blond bluegrass boundaries-pusher is Patty Loveless, a.k.a. the coal miner's daughter from Kentucky who is not

Loretta Lynn. Although Patty has had luck with up-tempo contemporary hits such as "I Try to Think About Elvis," she's got a mountain soul. "My father loved the mountain/bluegrass sounds of the Stanley Brothers, Lester Flatt and Earl Scruggs, and Bill Monroe," Patty explains. She can still remember her dad taking her to see Flatt, Scruggs, and the Foggy Mountain Boys do a gig at her local theater when she was six years old.

Invited to play a Ralph Stanley bluegrass festival back in 1993, Patty quickly assembled a group playing banjo, upright bass, mandolin, dobro, and fiddle. Her producer-husband, Emory Gordy Jr., played guitar and helped adapt her hits "The Lonely Side of Love" and "Don't Toss Us Away" for bluegrass instrumentation. For her 2001 return-to-roots album, *Mountain Soul,* Patty put her own spin on the *O Brother* signature tune, singing that she's a "Soul of Constant Sorrow." It works just as well as a girl song as it does as a Soggy Bottom Boys lament.

We Want Dolly

Unlike the other blondes who are pushing bluegrass to bigger and better levels, Dolly Parton was actually drafted into service. Sugar Hill Records did a market research survey, asking people which artist they would be most interested in hearing tackle the genre. The name that came up most often was Parton's. They were right; Dolly kicks out the jams as a bluegrass-and-then-

some artist. Not only does she do her own compositions, she's fearless about adapting completely left-of-field choices such as MTV-staple Collective Soul's "Shine" and Led Zeppelin's "Stairway to Heaven."

Dolly did bring in ringers, asking Alison Krauss, Union Station, Nickel Creek, and Patty Loveless to help her out. All considered it a privilege. Alison even goes so far as to say Dolly Parton singing is what she images heaven must sound like. Parton laughs about how she's reached new artistic heights by returning to her mountain roots. "I had to get rich in order to afford to sing like I was poor again!"

Alison Krauss + Union Station, *Live* (Rounder)—Two CDs, twenty-five songs. Recorded live in Louisville, this is everyone's new favorite!

Various Artists, *O Brother, Where Art Thou? Soundtrack* (Mercury)—Remember the three sirens in the stream? Voices provided by Alison Krauss, Emmylou Harris, and Gillian Welch.

Various Artists, *The Best of Bluegrass, 20th Century Masters: The Millennium Collection* (Hip-O)—Hear the original masters, with "newcomers" Vince Gill and Ricky Skaggs thrown in as well.

Elvis Presley, *The Million Dollar Quartet* (BMG)—Elvis and the boys do snatches of four Bill Monroe compositions: "Little Cabin Home on the Hill," "Summertime Is Past and Gone," "I Hear a Sweet Voice Calling," and "Sweetheart, You Done Me Wrong."

Nickel Creek, *Nickel Creek* (Sugar Hill)—Can these three kids be any more fab? We think not!

Patty Loveless, *Mountain Soul* (Epic)—Patty starts off strong with "The Boys Are Back in Town," a swell song exhorting girls to get ready for the country equivalent of Fleet Week.

Dolly Parton, *Halos and Horns* (Sugar Hill)—A stairway to heaven.

Chapter **5**

Treasure Hunting
at the Hall of Fame

Recently moved into their fancy new building, Nashville's Country Music Hall of Fame and Museum is one-stop shopping for girls interested in the past, present, and future of country music. We're signed up for a private Girls' Guide tour, but apparently, we're a dozen years too late. If we had come prior to 1991, our tour guide might have been Trisha Yearwood!

"We've had many people who've worked here who've become stars," reports Diana Johnson, vice president of Museum Services. "Trisha Yearwood worked in the store and as a tour guide, then went from here to her record deal. Kathy Mattea is another who quit to pursue singing."

Trisha's employment application form is one of the artifacts Diana points out to us. There are so many great treasures
on display and so much historical information to absorb that
we've asked Diana to single out five objects that are easy to overlook but that girls might particularly enjoy.

Carter Scratch Fever

Diana: "Mother Maybelle Carter's guitar is probably
one of the six most important artifacts we've got,
and probably one of the most important in the
history of country music—in all music—because
it has influenced so many people. Everybody
who plays guitar uses the Mother Maybelle style
one time or another, even if they're not aware
that's what they're doing. It's amazing when you
consider that she bought that guitar and started
using it in the 1920s."

To put Mother Maybelle into historical context, picture the
scene in *O Brother, Where Art Thou?* when George Clooney and his
two stooges stumble across a man who wants to record them.
Well, neither Maybelle's brother-in-law A. P. Carter nor Jimmie Rodgers (a.k.a. "The Singing Brakeman") was Clooney

handsome, but both men were discovered by Ralph Peer at a similar cattle call recording session in Bristol, Tennessee, in 1927. This was five years after the Victor Talking Machine Company recorded "Sallie Gooden" with fiddler Eck Robertson, which was the very first country record ever made. Yet the Bristol Sessions are considered to be the birth of the country music industry, with Jimmie Rodgers labeled "The Father of Country Music" and the Carters "The First Family."

A. P. Carter's band consisted of himself, his wife, Sara, and his brother's wife, Maybelle (who was also Sara's cousin). Recording more than three hundred songs during their reign from 1927 to 1943, the Carter Family did both originals and traditionals, including "Can the Circle Be Unbroken," "Wildwood Flower," and "Wabash Cannonball." In the 1950s, Mother Maybelle headed up a second-generation Carter Family consisting of her daughters Helen, Anita (whom young Elvis lusted after), and June (whom Johnny Cash married). June's daughter Carlene Carter and stepdaughter, Rosanne Cash, round out a third generation.

In addition to giving birth to talented Carter girls, Mother Maybelle birthed a distinctive guitar style that is now known as "the Carter Scratch." Having first learned the autoharp and then the five-string banjo, Mother Maybelle saw no reason why she couldn't play the guitar by using her thumb to pluck the bass strings while her fingers brushed the higher strings. Most modern-day guitarists use this easy technique to play melody and rhythm at the same time without knowing what they're doing is the Carter Scratch.

Pre-Boot Scootin' Boogie

Diana: "Patsy Montana was able to combine 'country' and 'western' better than anybody else—and she put a rocking beat in her songs long before rock and roll came on the scene. The Patsy Montana cowgirl boots on display are just terrific. Even if they didn't belong to her, the boots are real collector's items because they're so intricately carved out of the leather."

With the Great Depression in full swing, Patsy Montana sat down and wrote herself an upbeat song that captured a woman's longing to escape reality. Decked out in her now famous boots and a fringed cowgirl dress, Patsy Montana strummed her guitar as fast as she could and yodeled her way through "I Want to Be a Cowboy's Sweetheart." Depression-weary women bought into the romantic fantasy, and the 1935 record became the first by a female country singer to sell a million copies.

Women in the post–*Urban Cowboy* era also embraced the fantasy when Suzy Bogguss revived Patsy's song decades later. The

Dixie Chicks also covered "Sweetheart" in their early cowgirl years. True heirs to Montana, the Chicks also penned their own cowboy wish-fulfillment song, "Cowboy, Take Me Away."

An American Beauty

Diana: "Emmylou Harris got to know us because she came here to research the Louvin Brothers in the seventies. We have Emmylou's first rose guitar, which she gave to us a very long time ago. She's had others made up since then, but on display is the Gibson guitar with the inlaid rose that she had from the moment she could afford it."

Emmylou Harris comes from the generation that idolized Joan Baez, Judy Collins, and others in the Bob Dylan folk scene. Gram Parsons recruited Emmylou to join the country-rock movement in 1972 (he died a year later), and ever since she's been credited for being the first to bring a young, rock-oriented audience to country.

After several albums in the country-rock vein, Emmylou moved into a more pure-country sound, then to bluegrass, gospel, Americana, and frankly anything that struck a chord with her. She's collaborated with everyone from Johnny Cash to Steve Earle, John Denver to Lyle Lovett. And let's not forget her incredible eye for spotting talent. Members of her Hot Band who have gone on to become major Nashville players include Ricky Skaggs, Vince Gill, Rodney Crowell, producer Emory Gordy Jr., and record label honcho Tony Brown.

⋆ Rare Hair Treasure *⋆*

Diana: "The Dolly Parton costume and wig on display date back to the 1980s. It's an interesting period for Dolly. I think she would be the first to say it's one of her tackiest periods, and she's proud of that! Not that she's actually reached the pinnacle of her career, because she keeps reinventing herself (yet she stays the same in the oddest way), but this costume was worn during the period when she was selling a huge amount of records. More importantly, she brought huge numbers of fans to country music who never considered listening to it before.

"This is the first place outside of her own museum that Dolly has allowed anyone to display a wig, because she is very picky about that sort of thing and because they can look weird floating by themselves headless. Dolly actually came over here and walked us through what she wanted to have happen. She had great ideas, frankly.

"People are so overwhelmed by Dolly's persona that they don't understand she's a serious, talented woman. I think a hundred years from now people will remember her songs more than anything else. To me, Dolly does the perfect country song because all of her songs tell stories. What separates country music from most other types of music in the world is the storytelling aspect of it. It tells a story, it has a moral. Whether it's a contemporary person or a person from the 1920s, that's the thread, that tradition of storytelling."

Criticized for ditching her country sound when she achieved mainstream success, Dolly Parton shot back that she wasn't leaving country behind, she was taking it with her to new places. Reputed to have written over three thousand songs, Dolly's given the world "Dumb Blonde," "Jolene," "Coat of Many Colors," "Here You Come Again," and the unstoppable "I Will Always Love You."

While no one would deny the importance of Jimmie Rodgers, Hank Williams, or even Garth Brooks, nobody in country music has ever been as famous or has had such worldwide success as the poor Tennessee mountain girl with big hair and even bigger boobs. "If country had its own money," fan Bear Fisher theorizes, "Dolly would be on the dollar bill."

⁺⋆⁺ Y'All Come Back and See Us! ⁺⋆⁺

Diana: "On your way out, don't forget to look for Trisha Yearwood's application to work at the museum. It's near the exit!"

Thanks, Diana! We look forward to returning when we can spend more time. Patsy Cline's makeup case definitely merits a second look.

Trisha Yearwood, *Trisha Yearwood* (MCA)—Trisha's self-titled first album includes the now classic "She's in Love with the Boy." Don't miss Garth Brooks harmonizing on "Like We Never Had a Broken Heart."

Various Artists, *Country: The American Tradition / Sony Music 100 Years Soundtrack for a Century* (Columbia/Epic/Legacy)—A two-disk, fifty-one-song overview. The Carter Family's "Can the Circle Be Unbroken" is track number eight, immediately followed by Patsy Montana's cowboy ditty.

Various Artists, *Will the Circle Be Unbroken* (Capitol)—The Nitty Gritty Dirt Band gets Mother Maybelle and other greats to dish up classics. Make sure to check out the *Circle* sequels, Vols. II–III.

Various Artists, *The Songs of Jimmie Rodgers—A Tribute* (Egyptian/Columbia)—Modern artists cover the Father of Country Music's signature tunes. Alison Krauss + Union Station take on "Any Old Time," Mary Chapin Carpenter impresses with "Somewhere Down Below the

Mason Dixon Line," and Iris DeMent warbles "Hobo Bill's Last Ride."

Emmylou Harris, *Profile/Best of Emmylou Harris* (Warner Bros.)—In this 1978 collection, Emmylou sings songs written by A. P. Carter, the Louvin Brothers, Buck Owens, Delbert McClinton, Carlene Carter, Chuck Berry, and Dolly Parton. Is this woman eclectic, or what?

Dolly Parton, Linda Ronstadt, Emmylou Harris, *Trio* (Warner Brothers)—What a threesome. If you like this one, there's a sequel as well (*Trio II*).

Dolly Parton, *The Best of Dolly Parton* (Camden)—Everything from "Jolene" to "9 to 5," with a cover of "Harper Valley P.T.A." thrown in for extra kitsch value.

Chapter 6

Record Shopping
with Pam Tillis

I t's easy to get overwhelmed by eight decades' worth of music for sale at Nashville's famous Ernest Tubb Record Shop. Founded in 1947 by the legendary singer, the store continues to stock hard-to-find records along with the most recent releases. With the work of so many great artists at our fingertips, we don't even know where to begin. Luckily, we've roped Pam Tillis into giving us some recommendations. Not only is Pam a terrific writer and singer in her own right (with a whole catalog of great girl songs, including "Cleopatra, Queen of Denial," "Mi Vida Loca [My Crazy Life]," and "Spilled Perfume"), she recently dipped into her father Mel's catalog to record *It's All Relative—Tillis*

Sings Tillis. Excluding her own and her father's music, we asked Pam to suggest some classics that will, in Pam's words, "do our hearts a lot of good."

No Consumer Disequilibrium

Pam introduces us to this concept. "That means when you go to the record store to buy a rock-and-roll record, you want to buy a straight-up rock-and-roll record. When you buy a country record, you want to know what you're getting."

She elaborates, "I don't think any music exists in a vacuum. I don't think country music should stay stuck in the past. I don't even have a big beef with crossover. There's a place for all of it. But when they try to pass something off as country that's nowhere near country, then it seems a little deceptive. The day they stop putting fiddles and steel guitars or mandolins anywhere on a country record I don't know why you would need to buy it or call it country."

We asked Pam what she likes about country. "Believe me, you're talking to somebody who has gone through every different kind of musical phase, loves everything from the most popular— music so popular that it could be a gum commercial—to the most obscure, and everything in between. Sometimes just the basic-ness of country music sounds so soothing, so comforting.

"At times pop lyrics can be a little oblique. I love a great straight-ahead lyric. I grew up with great country songwriting where it's all about lyrics, where sometimes the music is kind of almost secondary. I love a great story in a song."

On Your Mark, Get Set, Go!

With no direction other than to list some classic artists that girls should have in their record collection, we let Pam Tillis loose.

Pam: "Yesterday when I was in the Gap, they were playing a real cool mix of music and they played an old Hank Williams thing. I know there's more to country music than Hank Williams, don't get me wrong. But just check out 'Move It on Over,' and listen to the lyrics. It's just so great! So **Hank Williams** is almost the primer.

"And of course **Patsy Cline**.

"**Marty Robbins** was a fabulous singer.

"**Ray Price** has got a new album out. Ray Price is as good as Ray Price ever was.

"Some of the stuff my twenty-three-year-old son loves is **Ernest Tubb, Lefty Frizzell,**

Carl Smith, Hank Thompson, Hank Snow.
That's kind of my dad's era.

"**Roger Miller** is an unbelievable
songwriter. Just unbelievable! Some of it's
real off the wall, and you just don't think of
them as being that adventurous back then.

"**Johnny Cash!**

"**The Everly Brothers.** In their era, they
were actually considered pop and rock, but
there's a purity there that, to me, is very
country. I love them. The early Everlys are
unbelievable.

"Of course, the biggies, **Loretta, Tammy.**
But go listen to something different. Like check
out some **Jeannie Seely** or **Jean Shepard,** or
some less-well-known singers who are Opry stars.

"Early **Willie Nelson**—so hip!

"**Kris Kristofferson.**

"**Merle Haggard.**

"Something really raw and early, like
Jimmie Rodgers.

"**Emmylou Harris**—everything Emmylou
Harris ever did is essential.

"Another person with a great country voice
that I did a show with not too long ago is **Gene
Watson.** Gene is a great singer!

"Did you catch the *CMT 40 Greatest Women
of Country Music* special? They put **Barbara
Mandrell** down at thirty-eight. I was like, are
you kidding me?! Barbara Mandrell had the
first major television show of a female artist!
Any woman who won Entertainer of the Year,
you need to know what they were up to because
that's almost as hard as, well, I don't know what!

"Unless you get the satellite channels that
play classic country, it's like the country music
industry doesn't even remember these people
exist. Don't get me started!"

Pam Tillis, *It's All Relative—Tillis Sings Tillis* (Lucky Dog)—
Discover Mel Tillis's greatness through Pam's tribute.

Hank Williams, *40 Greatest Hits* (Polydor)—Hank
Williams is America's Shakespeare. Like the Bard,
Hank's songs are accessible, timeless, entertaining,
and meaningful to generation after generation.

Ray Price, *Time* (Audium Entertainment)—When Willie
Nelson asked his friends to sing along with him on a
2002 television special, Nelson made sure to include
Ray Price. Price's 2002 album finds the seventy-
something singer in excellent voice.

Ernest Tubb, *The Last Sessions—All Time Greatest Hits*
(First Generation)—Find out why Junior Brown has
a song called "My Baby Don't Dance to Nothing But
Ernest Tubb."

Johnny Cash, *Now Here's Johnny Cash* (Sun Records)—
Enjoy vintage Cash, back when he was Elvis's label
mate on Sun.

The Everly Brothers, *All-Time Original Hits* (Rhino
Records)—Rediscover young Don and Phil as country
crooners.

Barbara Mandrell, *Ultimate Collection* (Hip-O Records)—
Forget about the glitzy TV appearances, give the lady a
little respect as a serious hitmaker. Did we mention
Barbara was once upon a time a steel guitar–playing
child prodigy?

Chapter **7**

The Loretta Lynn
School of Success

When Loretta Lynn agreed to appear on A&E's *Live by Request* in 2001, she must have secretly worried no one would call in. How many people still care about an artist who made her first record in 1960? Loretta had no reason to fear. The show logged in over one million phone calls. Everyone loves the coal miner's daughter. Johnny Cash, when inducting her into the Country Music Hall of Fame in 1988, called Loretta one of the most admired women of our time.

In 1980, a film version of Loretta's autobiography, *Coal Miner's Daughter,* was released with Sissy Spacek as Loretta and Tommy Lee Jones as her husband, Doo. Aspiring superstars,

go to the nearest Blockbuster and rent it. Because not only is it a terrific movie, it functions as a blueprint for success in the country music field. However, those who dare to follow in Mrs. Lynn's footsteps, be warned! Loretta admitted on CMT's *Inside Fame* that she never would have embarked on her singing career if she had known what the future would bring.

⋅⁺* How to Be a Country Superstar *⁺⋅ in Fourteen Easy Steps

Step 1: Decide to become a singer.

A housewife with four small children, Loretta embarked upon her career because her husband liked the way she sang to "the babies." If, like Loretta, you find yourself committed to being a wife and mother before starting your career, don't despair. While it's true Faith Hill, Shania Twain, and the various Dixie Chicks became moms after gold records hung on their walls, Lee Ann Womack had her first daughter before she got her MCA deal.

Step 2: Get some club experience.

Loretta's husband, Doo, talked the local honky-tonk house band into letting her join them. Local clubs still provide a solid training ground. Before even thinking about moving to Nashville, you should get some performing experience close to home. Any venue will suffice. Garth Brooks remembers the first place he performed was an Oklahoma City pizza joint called Shotgun Sam's, where he played six hours a night, four nights a week, and had to pay for his own pizza!

Step 3: Write a song.

Having no clue where singers find songs, Loretta realized she better come up with her own. After spending many nights in honky-tonks, she had the inspiration to write "Honky-Tonk Girl." Like many country songs, Loretta's hit tune only had three chords: I, IV, V. The late legendary country songwriter Harlan Howard once proclaimed a country song is "three chords and the truth." Keeping Mr. Howard's advice in mind, you should write a song that is specific to your own experience but one to which others can relate as well. After all, the best country songs are rooted in the personal but resonate universally. Keep it simple and honest (two hallmarks of great country songs).

Remember, writing remains an excellent way to get your foot in the door. Canadian Carolyn Dawn Johnson came to Nashville with a game plan of writing songs for others, then getting her own record deal. Penning the number-one hit "Single White Female" for singer Chely Wright put single-white-female Carolyn on the map.

Step 4: Make a record.

Loretta's husband arranged for her to make her first recording on a shoestring budget. Although singers get signed from live showcases, you should always have something recorded to demonstrate your singing ability (i.e., a demo). The good news is that with the proliferation of home recording studios, it's never been easier to make demos.

If you're lucky enough to get a record deal, don't think you're home free. In recent years, many artists have been hampered by their labels' going out of business before their records were released. Chris Cagle, for example, was a victim of Virgin Records Nashville closing its doors before his *Play It Loud* CD could debut. Luckily, Capitol picked up the project and ran with it.

Step 5: Get airplay.

The movie shows that Loretta and her husband employed a very mom-and-pop approach. After sending out a personalized letter, photograph, and record to every disc jockey in the nation, the Lynns piled into their car and visited stations in person. One DJ told the couple Loretta's record flopped with listeners, which they believed until Loretta spotted her record unopened in a stack of submissions.

Sadly, the days of asking disc jockeys to give your unknown record a trial spin are long gone. You'll notice in CD liner notes and on award shows country stars always thank "country radio" for supporting them—not individual stations or disc jockeys, but the format as a whole. Today's radio is big business, with most stations owned by big conglomerates like Clear Channel and conservatively programmed according to market research.

Step 6: Get a hit single.

Loretta and Doo's mom-and-pop approach resulted in a hit single. In today's marketplace, it's practically impossible to get a hit without a record company putting major promotional support behind your song and radio putting it into heavy rotation.

Kenny Chesney is an example of an artist who understands the importance of picking songs that have radio potential. He admits to recording "a bunch of songs that I knew I could probably get up the chart." If you're interested in the magic formula, Alan Jackson spells it out in the title of one of his "shame on you, music industry" tunes that he loves to lob out occasionally: "Three-Minute Positive Not Too Country Up-Tempo Love Song."

Step 7: Pay your dues.

When success came fast for Loretta, she worried that she hadn't paid her dues. But if you can become a star without struggling, more power to you! Still, even the youngest singers have usually spent some time behind the microphone before hitting it big. Teen sensation Jessica Andrews, who auditioned for Nashville super producer Byron Gallimore at the age of twelve, had previously logged in hours at elementary school talent shows.

Step 8: Play the Grand Ole Opry.

Loretta proclaimed her Opry debut the highlight of her life. You know you've been accepted by the country world when you debut on the Grand Old Opry. The longest-running continuously aired radio program in America (it began on station WSM in 1925), the Opry isn't quite the same as it was in its heyday, but performers still consider it a big deal to play and to become members. In addition to being broadcast on radio, a televised version airs every Saturday night on CMT. Watch it to check out your competition!

Step 9: Plan carefully what you're going to do next.

Having no background in artist management, Loretta's husband winged it. Certainly your husband can promote your gigs as you begin your career, but today's stars have professional managers to pilot theirs. That's not to say that many of today's heavy hitters don't have mates actively involved behind the scenes. John McBride used to work Garth Brooks concerts (while undiscovered Martina manned Garth's T-shirt booth); he now runs his wife's tours. Reba McEntire's spouse is her partner in all facets of her career while Shania Twain is married to her cowriter/producer (as is Patty Loveless).

Step 10: Make friends with bigger stars who can help your career.

Loretta's patron saints were established stars Ernest Tubb and Patsy Cline (who became one of her dearest friends). You should take advantage of the fact that country stars are willing to help newcomers. If you can, get Alan Jackson's patronage. Alan loved debut artist Lee Ann Womack's song "Never Again, Again" so much that he bought dozens of copies of her first CD and

talked her up everywhere. He's still championing her, even though she's now a big star in her own right. When Alan performed "Golden Rings" on the Grand Ole Opry, guess who did Tammy's part.

Step 11: Tour incessantly.

Loretta traveled by bus as she crossed the nation doing her concert tours. You'll discover that touring is the lifeblood of a country singer. Clint Black claims the Lone Star state is so heavily populated with live music venues that up-and-coming musicians can easily tour the state for over a decade and never play the same joint twice. Even when you become a headliner, you'll remain a road warrior. Although the miles add up, so do the ticket sales. An artist like Tim McGraw can pull in nearly $25 million a year when he tours.

Step 12: Put career in high gear, sacrificing quality of life, health, and family time.

Loretta was away from home so much that she sometimes had trouble telling her twins apart! Super-stardom will take its toll, but you will figure out how to avoid the pitfalls. Many stars, for instance, take their kids on the road. Martina McBride, whose husband works with her, brings her daughters on tour. Tim and Faith also pack their babies on the bus. Even Garth tried to haul his family with him before deciding he better retire to spend more time with his daughters at home.

Step 13: Take time off.

Loretta retreated home to her Hurricane Mills ranch. Taking time off is always a good way to regroup and replenish your artistic inspiration. Not too long ago, Faith, Shania, and the Dixie Chicks took extended breaks (all were busy producing babies). The superstars' sabbaticals were actually a boon for country music, allowing developing artists such as Chris Cagle, Rascal Flatts, SHeDAISY, and Trace Adkins to fill the vacuum. The superstars then returned with albums (*Cry, Up!* and *Home,* respectively) that stretched them in new creative directions.

Step 14: Repeat as many times as necessary.

Although she took many years off to be with her husband while he was terminally ill, Loretta is once again back in the recording studio and on tour. She's even written a sequel autobiography called *Still Woman Enough*. Loretta Lynn continues to be an inspiration to us all.

Loretta Lynn, *Still Country* (Audium Entertainment)—Widow Loretta's 2000 comeback album includes a tribute to her late husband, Doo, entitled "I Can't Hear the Music." Quite a change from her "Your Squaw Is on the Warpath" days!

Loretta Lynn, *20th Century Masters: The Best of Loretta Lynn (Millennium Collection)* (Universal)—Doesn't include "The Pill" but has most of her feisty female anthems.

Various Artists, *Coal Miner's Daughter Soundtrack* (MCA)—Sissy sings! If you were at singer Chely Wright's 2002 Fan Fair party, you know that Loretta Lynn and Sissy Spacek are still buds.

Chely Wright, *Single White Female* (MCA)—Not only is she a great singer, Chely is a huge Loretta Lynn fan.

Various Artists, *Grand Ole Opry 75th Anniversary, Vol. II* (MCA)—This and its predecessor are solid representations of the venerated institution.

Lee Ann Womack, *Lee Ann Womack* (MCA)—Play the tune that drives Alan Jackson wild.

Alan Jackson, *When Somebody Loves You* (Arista)— Songwriters who want to make it big quick, listen to Alan! Although he's being sarcastic, "Three-Minute Positive Not Too Country Up-Tempo Love Song" does delineate exactly what makes a song successful in today's country market.

Chapter **8**

Building the Perfect Country Star

As individual artists, singers Kix Brooks and Ronnie Dunn are fine. Together, they achieve excellence. Same thing with duo Eddie Montgomery and Troy Gentry and groups like Alabama, Lonestar, Diamond Rio, Trick Pony, or Rascal Flatts. The individual parts come together to make a superior whole.

That got us thinking, Tim McGraw is pretty darn near perfect, but he could be improved upon. What if you could take the best elements from artists currently working (perfect voice, perfect stage show, etc.) and put them together to fashion the ultimate country superstar? Sort of a Dream Team rolled into one superman. Tim McGraw, but the Six-Million-Dollar-Man version.

Hello, My Name Is

George Strait's real name is George Strait, but Shania's is Eileen. Faith got Hill from an early marriage, as did Patty Loveless (her ex's name was really Lovelace, but Patty made it more poetic). Garth dropped his given name Troyal, while Toby Keith ditched the surname Covel and Gary Allan discarded Herzberg. Clearly, there's room to wiggle when a person decides to become a recording artist. The best name in country music? Toby Keith says it's Merle Haggard. It's true that both "Merle" and "Haggard" practically scream "country" (and it's his real name!), but we lean toward the eternally cool Johnny Cash (insiders call him John or just Cash).

Perfect country name: John Carter Cash. The son of Johnny and June has the ultimate thoroughbred name.

Sopranos Need Not Apply

Merle Haggard and George Jones both sing baritone. Artists who claim Merle influenced the way they sing include Trace Adkins, Mark Chesnutt, Alan Jackson, Toby Keith, and Randy

Travis. But there's no denying George Jones's greatness. Lee Ann Womack says Jones's magic lies in the tone of his voice, the way he uses it, his phrasing.

Perfect country voice: George Jones. Loretta Lynn says George Jones is the greatest living country singer. Who can argue with Loretta?

He's a Poet and He Knows It

Blame it on Dylan. After Bob, we expect performers to write their own songs. While several country artists do, most rely on the professional songwriters who dominate Nashville. Hank Williams and Harlan Howard are indisputably the best songwriters country has produced, but they are no longer with us. Who is a worthy successor?

Perfect country songwriter: Bruce Springsteen. It's true, one doesn't think of the Boss as country, despite the fact that CMT plays his videos. But not only does Bruce craft great story songs, he's also a master at country staples such as love ballads, heartache reportage, workingman blues, and patriotic anthems. His tunes work for Faith Hill ("If I Should Fall Behind"), Kenny Chesney ("One Step Up"), Travis Tritt ("Tougher Than the Rest"), The Mavericks ("All That Heaven Will Allow"), Patty Griffin ("Stolen Car"), Steve Earle ("Nebraska," "State Trooper"), Chris LeDoux ("Tougher Than the Rest"), Trisha Yearwood ("Sad

Eyes"), Johnny Cash ("I'm on Fire," "Johnny 99"), and Emmylou Harris ("Mansion on the Hill," "My Father's House," "Across the Border"). Have no doubt that one hundred years from now country singers will still be covering the Boss.

Windows to the Soul

Frank Sinatra didn't do too badly with a pair of blue eyes. Neither have Trace Adkins, Garth Brooks, Kenny Chesney, Merle Haggard, Alan Jackson, Toby Keith, John Michael Montgomery, Eddie Montgomery, Collin Raye, Aaron Tippin, Randy Travis, Travis Tritt, or Dwight Yoakam.

Perfect country eyes: Garth Brooks. Garth works those peepers like nobody's business when he performs in concert. Everyone in the audience thinks GB is connecting with them directly. Brooks is also notorious for letting his eyes swell with tears anytime he talks about his hero, George Jones. In rock or rap, a man can't cry. But in country, you get extra points if you let your emotions show.

Dressed to Impress

From Hank Williams's Nudie suits to Johnny Cash's Man in Black ensemble, country singers have had signature looks. As much as people knock the "hat acts," when you see a guy stride on stage wearing a Stetson (or Resistol or Charlie One Horse) there's no doubt that he's a country singer.

Perfect country stage costume: Eddie Montgomery of Montgomery Gentry. From the bottom of his red boots to the top of his distinctive Charlie One Horse hat, Eddie has put together a classic yet modern Western look. It's clearly a stage costume,

but it doesn't look freaky out of context (like Elvis's jumpsuits did). More important, Eddie wears the suit, it doesn't wear him. Fans aren't horribly disappointed when he and T-Roy (as

Eddie likes to call partner Troy Gentry) perform in informal shorts and do-rags. But when the suit is donned, there's a certain something special happening.

I'd Pay to See That!

Garth Brooks is credited for bringing rock-and-roll concert theatrics to country music. Before Garth, country stars apparently never thought about flying over the audience. Now performers are expected to put on a grand show.

Perfect concert headliner: George Strait. The Amusement Business named his Country Music Festival the #1 Touring Country Act of the Decade (the nineties). Having figured out what the audience wants from him during his many years on the Texas bar circuit, George and his Ace in the Hole band serve up a solid set showcasing as many of his number-one hits as possible. Of course it doesn't hurt that his supporting acts are also stellar. Artists who have opened for Strait include Tim McGraw, Alan Jackson, Kenny Chesney, Brad Paisley, Jo Dee Messina, and the Dixie Chicks.

⋆ Purrfection *⋆*

Johnny's son's name, George J.'s voice, Bruce's words, Garth's eyes, Eddie's clothes, George S.'s act. What are we missing? Oh, right. Tim McGraw's sex appeal. That should do it.

Wait, what about creating the perfect female artist? That's already been done. She's got it all—the name (real), the looks (not real, but real country!), the voice, the songwriting, the sex appeal. Yes, we're talking about the one and only Miss Dolly Parton.

Johnny Cash, *Johnny Cash at Folsom Prison and San Quentin* (Columbia)—Leave it to Johnny to drag June along with him to prison. John Carter Cash's parents duet on "Jackson" and "Give My Love to Rose."

George Jones, *The Essential George Jones/The Spirit of Country* (Epic/Legacy)—A two-CD compilation of every George Jones song you'd ever want to hear including the one many people say is the finest country song ever recorded, "He Stopped Loving Her Today."

Various Artists, *Badlands: A Tribute to Bruce Springsteen's Nebraska* (Sub Pop)—Raul Malo turns "Downbound Train" into a Mavericks' song, Deana Carter kills with "State Trooper," and Hank Williams III makes "Atlantic City" sound like it was written just to be a country rave-up.

Garth Brooks, *Double Live* (Capitol)—We're not sure exactly where these tracks were recorded, since nothing on the CD indicates location. One thing's for sure, though, it wasn't Folsom Prison.

Montgomery Gentry, *My Town* (Columbia)—Tough guys Eddie and T-Roy stake their turf.

George Strait, *For the Last Time—Live From the Astrodome* (MCA)—George performs songs guaranteed to get your feet tapping.

Tim McGraw, *Greatest Hits* (Curb)—Sigh . . .

the TAMMY

Truly Outstanding Hair

The Academy of Country Music, Country Music Association, and even CMT are clueless. Every year they and countless other organizations dole out awards that recognize various achievements in country music while overlooking the most deserving category: truly outstanding hair.

Since there's clearly a void in the marketplace, *The Girls' Guide to Country* proposes to fill it with an award that in the tradition of the Grammy, Tony, and Emmy we shall call the Tammy—after the First Lady of Country Music, Tammy Wynette, a hairdresser turned superstar who kept her beautician's license current all her life.

Why hasn't someone previously created such a prize? It's true that Mother Maybelle Carter was better known for her revolutionary guitar playing than her librarianesque hairstyle, "Father of Country Music" Jimmie Rodgers was a committed cap wearer, and neither Hank Williams nor Patsy Cline had revolutionary 'dos. But you would have thought a Hairstyle Hall of Fame would have been instituted in the 1960s, 1970s, or 1980s, when country hair really was big.

While the general public still erroneously associates today's country music with the frozen-in-time hairdos still seen occasionally on the older Grand Ole Opry regulars, the truth is most of the current superstars have hairstyles that are very contemporary—and almost generic. In the "nice, but not noteworthy" category: Shania Twain, Trisha Yearwood, George Strait, and too many others to waste time listing. When people talk about such singers, their hair almost never gets mentioned.

On the opposite end of the spectrum are those performers whose hair indisputably defines their persona. If any of these singers were to change their hairstyles, not only would it be newsworthy but their fans would be devastated.

Some of these Tammy-worthy hairstyles are trendsetting, others trend-bucking. And yes, there's a mullet or two. But the point is these are signature heads of hair, equally as important as the artists' name or voice in establishing their identity.

Without any further ado, *The Girls' Guide to Country* nominates the following artists for the inaugural Tammy Award recognizing outstanding achievements in contemporary country hair. And the nominees in the female category are:

* ⋆ * ⋆ *Crystal Gayle* ⋆ * ⋆ *

Although two of her biggest hits referenced her peepers ("I've Cried [the Blue Right Out of My Eyes]" and "Don't It Make My Brown Eyes Blue"), Crystal Gayle is famous for her waterfall tresses.

Crystal knew she had her work cut out for her when she decided to follow her incredibly successful big sister Loretta Lynn into the music industry. Loretta helped Brenda Gayle Webb pick out a new name (in part because the record company already had a Brenda on the roster—Brenda Lee) and then strongly advised the newly minted Crystal Gayle to avoid recording Lynn-style music. This helped Crystal establish her own identity, but what also set her apart were her glamorous looks. How many coal miner's daughters look like that?!

While her heyday was the late 1970s and early 1980s, Crystal Gayle still performs over a hundred concerts annually and keeps her locks three inches off the ground to avoid accidents on stage. Oh sure, we could remind you that Crystal has almost three dozen hit records to her name and was the first female country artist to have a platinum-selling album (*We Must Believe in Magic*), but frankly all everyone talks about is that hair.

Dolly Parton

Dolly jokes that she doesn't know how long it takes to do her hair because she's never there when it's being styled. Because, of course, Ms. Parton wears wigs. Although it was recently discontinued, she even had her own wig line, which was praised for its high quality at reasonable prices. Among the styles offered: "Country Heart," "Memphis Belle," and "Sweet Dreams." Enjoying yet another renaissance in her career with a stripped-down, bluegrass sound, Dolly's current hairstyle is appropriately very natural-looking. That is to say, as natural-looking as Dolly Parton could ever be.

⋆⁺ Reba McEntire ⁺⋆

Here's one big difference between the twentieth-century and the twenty-first-century Reba McEntire: her hair. The old Reba had a head of cascading red curls that grew increasingly unmanageable in the years after she became a mom. Once Reba made the decision to go short, she loped the curls off in increments, going shorter, shorter, shorter until on her third volume of greatest hits, released in 2001, she's fully cropped.

Of course, Reba's transformation was noted and interpreted as another sign that she was leaving her country roots behind. And indeed she is no longer just Reba McEntire, red-headed country singer with 50 million in record sales to her name. Reba is now a Broadway star (she played the ultimate singing cowgirl in *Annie Get Your Gun*), a television star (her self-titled WB series), a motion picture actress (a gun nut in the cult favorite *Tremors*), and a best-selling author (her autobiography and *Comfort from a Country Quilt*).

Like Cher, Reba's not in denial about aging and has visited the plastic surgeon to keep herself in fighting shape. Now in her late forties and willing to admit that she could be cast as LeAnn Rimes's grandmother, Reba deserves kudos for adapting her look to fit her current reality.

⋆⁺ The Judds ⁺⋆

The other redheads who defined country music in the 1980s were Wynonna and Naomi Judd. Before they disbanded in 1991 because of Mama Judd's health problems, the matching-hued duo sold more than 20 million records and won five Grammys. Once freed from her mother's domination, Wynonna expressed her independence by doing whatever she wanted with her music (cranking up the rock, soul, and gospel) and her hair (crazy long extensions, multicolor highlights, going orange, going blond, going straight). But in the end, Wynonna always returns to the Judd color of choice, which Naomi cheerfully identifies as a shade of red "that doesn't exist in nature."

Jo Dee Messina

Country's current redheaded sensation is Jo Dee Messina, who actually cited her hair color as the reason a record label should sign her. Ambushing a Curb Records exec at Fan Fair in 1994, she pointed out that his label needed a redhead. Of course, Jo Dee had the voice and the songs to back up her bravado.

In fact, as a Curb recording artist with hit singles like "Bye Bye," "I'm Alright," "Lesson in Leavin'," and "Stand Beside Me," she became Billboard's Most Played Country Female Artist of

1999. Not afraid of the comparison, Jo Dee names fellow carrottops Bonnie Raitt and Reba McEntire as two of her favorite singers, and even agreed to be part of the Judds' Power to Change 2000 Reunion tour.

⋆⁺˟ Faith Hill ⋆⁺˟

Who was the most written about performer at the 2001 People's Choice Awards? Faith Hill, who unveiled that night possibly the worst new hairdo in the history of country music. It was so bad—both in color (too white) and in cut (choppy, not in a good way)—that people who don't even know who Faith Hill is felt the need to comment on it. What's even worse, it was done by a big-name stylist, Peter Savic, who has also worked on Madonna and Christina Aguilera.

Other than this one glaring faux pas (which perhaps wasn't such a misstep considering how much attention in the "non-country" world it got her), Faith's hair has been one of her major assets. When she released her first album, *Take Me as I Am,* in 1993, her hair was typical of blond singers at that time: big, curly, and natural-looking color. Trisha Yearwood had similar hair when she released her first self-titled album in 1991. The thing that spun Faith's image into a new direction was meeting her husband-to-be, Tim McGraw. Proclaiming "my life began when I met my husband," Mrs. McGraw became a whole new person, with a new short hair look. As her sales increased and her videos got more expensive, Faith continued to lay on the glamour and layer in the hair extensions. Nowadays, the one-time girl next door can easily be mistaken for a supermodel (in fact, she models for Cover Girl) and is the benchmark against which all country beauties are measured.

The Dixie Chicks

When the Dixie Chicks were all blondes, reviewers always felt the need to mention it. Judging from the number of country singers who reached for the peroxide bottle, everyone seemed to think this was the secret to achieving Dixie Chicks— or Faith Hill–level success. Sara Evans, Jessica Andrews, Lee Ann Womack, Chely Wright, Patty Loveless, and even Alison Krauss have toyed with lighter locks.

Meanwhile, the Dixie Chicks's Emily Robison confounded everyone with her decision to go darker. Why in the world would a Chick return to her natural hair color? What could it mean? Robison said it was a by-product of having time off after their second album. Kicking back at home, she didn't want to be constantly going to the hair salon to touch up her naturally dark roots. Emily's rebellion was a harbinger for the group's radical return-to-their-roots 2002 CD, *Home*.

SHeDAISY

While the Dixie Chicks are generally given the respect they deserve, poor SHeDAISY is often the scapegoat for everything that's wrong with today's country. Although their 1999 debut album, *The Whole SHeBANG*, went double platinum, the group gets flack for their manufactured name, songs ("Lucky 4 You [Tonight I'm Just Me]"), musical influences (Aretha Franklin,

Annie Lennox, Karen Carpenter, Heart, Bette Midler, Dolly Parton, and the Judds), and looks. Although the three sisters presumably have similar natural hair color, Kristyn, Kelsi, and Kassidy Osborn found their hook by becoming a threesome made up of a blonde, a brunette, and a redhead. It helped differentiate the girls, who switch off singing lead, and made the telegenic trio CMT favorites.

⁺ Emmylou Harris *⁺*

In direct contrast to the Osborn sisters, Emmylou Harris represents what's real about female country singers. "I think if I've done anything, I've somehow managed to survive by doing exactly what I wanted to do," Emmylou states in her official record company bio. "I think I got into music at a time that was very special. I was just successful enough to be given a license to do whatever I wanted and to be left alone."

In the 1970s, Emmylou Harris and other singers such as Rita Coolidge and Joan Baez had the long, dark, flowing hair that typified the "natural" women of that era. Now, in an era when practically no one has untreated hair, arguably the most respected woman in country music sports her gray hair with pride.

And the Tammy Goes To

Crystal Gayle. Talk about trademark hair! Like her songs, Crystal's hair achieved crossover popularity and today is used as a reference beyond country music. The Discovery.com website, for example, cites it to explain hair growth, stating that human head hair tends to grow one inch every eight to ten weeks, so "if Gayle's hair is sixty inches long," the site calculates, it takes five to six hundred weeks for a single strand of the singer's hair to reach maximum length.

Crystal Gayle, *Best of Crystal Gayle* (Rhino Records)—Guaranteed to make your brown eyes turn blue and your hair to grow one inch every eight to ten weeks.

Reba McEntire, *Greatest Hits Volume III—I'm a Survivor* (MCA)—Shorthaired Reba is just as good as ever.

The Judds, *Greatest Hits* (RCA/Curb)—Don't get in their way when this dynamic redheaded duo celebrates "Girls Night Out."

Jo Dee Messina, *Burn* (Curb)—Jo Dee is red hot.

Faith Hill, *Faith* (Warner Bros.)—At her perkiest.

SHeDAISY, *The Whole SHeBANG* (Lyric Street)—Those Osborn girls are so creative they even have their own way of capitalizing words.

Emmylou Harris, *Red Dirt Girl* (Nonesuch)—Emmylou gets down and dirty.

Chapter **10**

Mullets
and More

The Kentucky waterfall, Tennessee top hat, Mississippi grapevine, Alabama shag, or Missouri compromise—call it what you will, the mullet is the most mocked haircut in modern memory. While it's true that hockey players remain true to the 'do, the poster child for mullet-mania is Billy Ray Cyrus. BRC's world-famous head of hair might have grabbed all the headlines, but many country crooners have been devotees of the short-on-top, long-on-the-bottom style. While there are quite a few outrageous locks on country hunks, let's begin our examination of notable manly coifs with the most obvious.

⋆⁺ Billy Ray Cyrus ⁺⋆

Billy Ray Cyrus had that hair before he hit it big with "Achy Breaky Heart" in 1992. He actually had the song too, which he told record executives always got people up on their feet when he performed the Don Von Tress–penned tune in clubs. It was the record company that invented the actual dance and force fed the steps to the American public. And it was the record company that made the video that launched Billy Ray Cyrus's legendary mullet onto the unsuspecting world.

Billy Ray's hair became the tail that wagged the dog. Luckily, the PAX television show *Doc* came his way, and he was able to adopt a relatively more conservative look, mandated by playing a doctor on TV. But don't think the hunky heartthrob has forsaken his music along with his extreme hair. Although he has never been able to replicate the out-of-the-ballpark success of his first album, he has continued to release new music, including a terrific cover of "Harper Valley P.T.A." Sock it to 'em, Billy Ray!

⁺⁺ ⁺ Willie Nelson ⁺⁺ ⁺

Back when Willie first came to Nashville in the early 1960s, he wrote such hits as "Crazy" (for Patsy Cline) and "Hello Walls" (for Faron Young), hung out at Tootsie's Orchid Lounge with singer/songwriters Mel Tillis and Roger Miller, and was the squarest-looking man you've ever seen. It wasn't until 1975, when he decided to stop playing by the rules, turned scruffy, and branded himself a redheaded stranger and an outlaw, that Willie Nelson came into his own. His subsequent path has been completely unpredictable and musically adventurous (remember his surreal 1984 duet with Julio Iglesias, "For All the Girls

I've Loved Before"?). Still making vital music and touring extensively, Willie has the kind of career longevity that very few artists achieve. How many senior citizens still get played in regular rotation on CMT? Just Willie, dueting with Lee Ann Womack on "Mendocino County Line," both of them flaunting long flowing hair blowing in the Texas wind.

George Jones

George Jones is rumored to have a barber chair in his home and a hairdresser who comes every day to do his 'do. He's from a generation that does that sort of thing. The result is a head of hair that doesn't seem to have changed since he first grew out the crew cut he sported in the early years of his career. Even when he was Mr. Tammy Wynette, his hair remained the same.

It's fitting that Jones's look is so frozen in time that it has become timeless—his music is as well. "She Thinks I Still Care," "A Good Year for the Roses," "He Stopped Loving Her Today," and "Choices"—they all sound like they could have been recorded in the same year, instead of 1962, 1970, 1980, and 1999, respectively.

The indestructible head of hair also symbolizes the man himself, who, despite years of chaotic living, is still alive and kicking and enjoying his reputation as America's greatest living country singer.

Lyle Lovett

Huh? In Lyle Lovett's current official headshot, he's wearing a hat! Although certainly not as newsworthy as his oddball short-lived marriage to Julia Roberts, this is a pretty radical statement for a singer/songwriter whose Eraserhead coif was his first claim to fame.

Perhaps it's because people still put too much emphasis on his Kramer-like mop (or as his record company refers to it, his "shock of untamed hair") that Lyle is trying to deflect attention

from his idiosyncratic follicles to his equally idiosyncratic music. But according to E. Jean Carroll's 1994 *Esquire* profile, Lyle has other things to offer besides quirky tunes like "If I Had a Boat" and occasional cameos in Robert Altman movies. Ms. Carroll reported that word on the "girl vine" is that Julia's first husband is supposedly one of the most impressively endowed gents in the entertainment business. Guess Lyle Lovett's hair isn't the only thing supersized!

Marty Stuart

Marty Stuart is committed to that big-hair look, and girls love him for it. Dixie Chicks singer Natalie Maines was thrilled when Marty Stuart arrived for an informal writing session in full glory (he helped pen two songs, "Tortured, Tangled Heart" and "I Believe in Love," for the their album *Home*). Morelia of Manuel Exclusive Clothier (Marty's favorite duds dealership) confirms that "Marty Stuart always looks like Marty Stuart, even if he's just driving around town in a jeep."

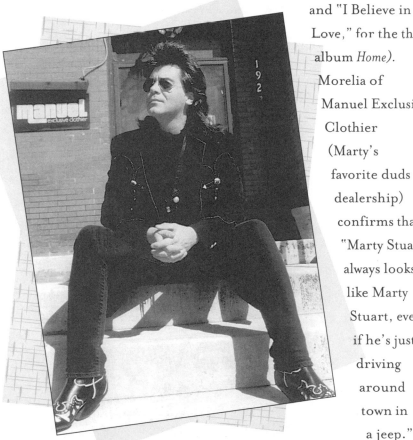

Known for his good taste in women (he married Johnny Cash's daughter Cindy and "Sweetheart of the Grand Ole Opry" Connie Smith) and extensive collection of country music clothing and artifacts, Marty got the most publicity of his career when he teamed up with equally hair-proud Travis Tritt on a series of singles ("The Whiskey Ain't Workin' " and "This One's Gonna Hurt You [for a Long, Long Time]") and the infamous 1992 No Hats Tour. With his unwavering commitment to high hair and Manuel glitz, Marty Stuart is a true believer in the old adage "If you've got it, flaunt it!"

⋆ Travis Tritt *⋆*

Travis Tritt can tell you the day he sold out: when he cut his hair at his record company's request. Back when he was signed in 1989, his label expected him to be an innocuous Gary Morris–type instead of the rebel heir to Duane Allman. The record company took a hard line, proclaiming Travis was doomed to failure if he fought their guidance. Suffering under the barber's shears, Travis realized nobody knew his look, his music, or his audience better than he. If he wanted to stay true to his artistic vision, he had to fight. Many years down the road, Travis remains the long-haired rebel carrying on the southern rock tradition.

˟˟ *Alan Jackson* ˟˟

Everyone talks about the night Alan Jackson performed George Jones's hit "Choices," instead of his own "Pop a Top," at the 1999 Country Music Association Award Show to protest the disgraceful way the televised show practiced ageism. Yes, it was a powerful moment. But didn't anybody notice how odd Alan looked with his normally scraggly blond curls tamed into a straightened ponytailed queue? It's equally disturbing watching the "Tonight I Climbed the Walls" video in which he is mustache-free. Alan Jackson isn't Alan Jackson without his blond curls and Magnum P.I. mustache. It's an outdated look, but it's been his look since his 1989 debut album, *Here in the Real World.* It fits the man whom everyone regards as a sincere traditionalist.

Garth Brooks

Garth Brooks would be the first to tell you he's not known for his hair. In fact, he's so not-hair-oriented that he doesn't even know what kind of shampoo he uses. And unlike other balding stars who refuse to show the world what's under their Stetson, Garth doffs his quite often and without fear. But when it came to creating an alter ego for his Chris Gaines project, the first thing Garth Brooks did was get himself some hair!

And the Tammy Goes To

After careful consideration, *The Girls' Guide to Country* awards the inaugural Tammy Award for outstanding achievement in contemporary country hair (male) to: Travis Tritt. Although Travis claims he isn't a "hair activist," how many other country performers can say, as Tritt does, that their hair symbolizes their artistic integrity? Travis has recently undergone some reimaging, cutting back on the leather and donning Italian-cut shirts. He's even trimmed his hair to a more manageable length. But rest assured, he'll never give up that Travis Tritt look.

Billy Ray Cyrus, *Best of Billy Ray Cyrus: Cover to Cover* (Polygram)—Modest BRC puts "Achy Breaky Heart" last on this compilation.

Willie Nelson, *The Great Divide* (Lost Highway)— The album cover shows his two trademarks: his hair and his much-worn guitar.

George Jones, *The Rock: Stone Cold Country 2001* (BMG/ Bandit)—No one doubts Mr. Jones remains Stone Cold Country. Don't miss Garth Brooks singing with his hero on "Beer Run (B Double E Double Are You In?)."

Lyle Lovett, *Anthology, Vol. I: Cowboy Man* (Curb/MCA)—With hat, without his large band. An impressive retrospective of Lyle's early recording career.

Marty Stuart, *20th Century Masters—The Millennium Collection: The Best of Marty Stuart* (MCA)—On the cover, they put the album title over his hair!

Travis Tritt, *Strong Enough* (Columbia)—What's the focal point on the cover of Travis's 2002 album? You guessed it. There's even back lighting on his locks for emphasis.

Chris Gaines, *Greatest Hits* (Capitol)—Don't be put off by the wig. Garth's odd one-off is actually a pretty decent album.

Chapter 11

Dixie Chic

Patsy Montana's cowgirl boots are museum pieces. Kitty Wells's gingham frock is packed away in storage. Even Lee Ann Womack's blue jeans have been banished to the back of the closet. What does it take to make the grade in the post–Shania Twain world? Music Row image consultant Renee Fowler and fashion columnist Nicole Melton reveal all.

A New Millennium

"Gone are the days when female country music artists lagged behind in fashion, as far as being out of sync with anyone else," proclaims Nicole Melton, who pens "Nicole's Style Notes" for

Country Music Today magazine. "I'm not really sure they were ever that out of sync. But now they're as current as any other genre you can match them up against."

Nicole adds, "It's the new millennium, and people have this perception that female country artists still have that big huge hair from the 1970s and 1980s. No!"

Good-bye to Western clothes and permed hair, hello to Faith Hill on the cover of *In Style, Marie Claire,* and *Jane.* How did this happen? Shania Twain rewrote the rule book and stylists ran with the ball.

"What the Hell's a Midriff?"

While guest-hosting on CMT, singer Eddie Montgomery stumbled over the scripted introduction to a Shania Twain video. Not the kind of guy who pays attention to fashion, Eddie had never heard the word "midriff" before. Shania herself has no clue why people still feel the need to discuss her bared stomach. She's not the first to don a cropped top (remember Madonna in the eighties?), but her decision to wear belly button—revealing clothes had a ripple effect in country music.

People magazine reporter Beverly Keel made a study of female stars' publicity photos before Shania and after. "Before, Faith Hill was the girl next door. Martina McBride was very high button, romantic blouses. Trisha Yearwood, also high necked. After

Shania, it got very sexy immediately. It probably would have gone that way anyway, it just would have taken much longer."

"That midriff phase is kind of over anyway," points out fashion columnist Nicole Melton. "That isn't the thing to do anymore, even if you wanted to."

·* Secrets from the ·* Chicks' Glam Squad

Image consultant Renee Fowler helped the Dixie Chicks ditch their cowgirl duds and climb into Todd Oldham. "When they first signed to Sony, they were Texas girls standing on a street corner in a little plaid skirts and cowboy boots. And we took them completely out of that. Because they're so lively, so bubbly, so vibrant—and their music talent is outrageous—I saw them more like that. Lots of color. And modern. We had several designers we worked with the Chicks at the beginning. Todd Oldham created a lot of their award show outfits, as well as their tour stuff for *Wide Open Spaces.* We also worked with Anna Sui a lot, also Vivienne Tam."

Todd Oldham, who is a Texan like the Chicks, punctuated their 1999 Grammy dresses with safety pins. "You all can't say we're not hip now," lead singer Natalie Maines told reporters crowding the red carpet.

"You know, I caught a lot of flack for the new Dixie Chicks image," confesses Renee. "I got calls from *Country Music Magazine* and other publications asking me why I would take women out of the country look. And my response is: A country look doesn't make country music. That depends on the way the artists portray themselves musically. It doesn't have anything to do with the actual visual. It really doesn't."

⋅⋆˙ That Don't Impress Me Much ˙⋆⋅

At the same 1999 award ceremony, Shania Twain was asked if it annoys her that people ask about her Marc Bouwer gown instead of her music. She admitted it didn't offend her because she considers fashion the fun part of her job.

While some people think award shows are just about awards, girls know it's also about the red carpet. No one remembers a week later who won what, but they remember what Faith Hill wore that night. Faith, who has also been known to wear Marc Bouwer along with Richard Tyler and Versace, always dresses like a movie star.

"Once an artist gets established, when they're attending award shows, performing on award shows, you can get a little more relaxed about what they wear to those things," says image consultant Renee Fowler. "But that's after an artist is established.

At the beginning, I would say for the first two years, for a new artist, it's really important that they stick close to what their image is."

On Shania's first album, the misguided record company bundled the Canadian diva up like Nanook of the North. That album barely sold. For the second album, Shania took control and hired Bo Derek's husband, John Derek, to shoot the photos (with Bo as his assistant). John Derek had imaged and styled his previous wives Ursula Andress and Linda Evans before people used "image" and "style" as verbs. He worked similar magic on Shania.

Music videos are where Shania's image came into sharp focus. Who can forget the girl in head-to-toe leopard print prowling the desert for a guy worthy of her attention? That was Marc Bouwer's take on Ms. Twain as Little Red Riding Hood. Shania was so impressed with the look that she wore the coat on several other occasions.

"The most important part is to be true to who you are," Renee Fowler counsels artists. "If you're trying to go after something and it feels uncomfortable, then it's not you."

For her Come on Over concert tour, Shania needed a stage outfit that could survive her high-energy show. And although she learned how to sing and walk down staircases wearing beaded gowns and high heels during her early years doing Vegas-style reviews in Canada, she opted this time for sneakers, cropped tops, and bellbottom pants. One of those outfits was auctioned off to benefit VH1 Save the Music Foundation. It pulled in $6,600 to help to restore music education in public schools.

⋅⋆⋆ *Want to Look Like a Star?* ⋅⋆⋆

Image consultant Renee Fowler says, "I think everybody targets a certain market. Younger girls are the Chicks' biggest audience draw, and I believe the Chicks hit their market to a T. What they wear really, really connects with their audience."

For girls who want to capture that *Wide Open Spaces* look, Renee suggests visiting your local Rampage. "Instead of Anna Sui, walk into a Rampage and pull every piece of color imaginable. Actually, we use a lot of that for photo shoots for new artists because it shoots so well. Might not be the highest quality, but it definitely, definitely works. It's what young girls need anyway, because it's trendy. Also, if you're good at picking through things, try Anthropologie. Shoe-wise, if you want to capture some of the things the younger new artists are doing, Steve Madden."

Fashion columnist Nicole Melton adds, "At a store like bebe, you can find some things similar to what artists have in their closet. When you want to get a little more juiced up, Betsey Johnson stores have clothing with a little bit of star dazzle." Nicole's best advice: "Peruse those sale racks!"

Lee Ann Womack, *Some Things I Know* (MCA)—Back in 1998, Lee Ann wore jeans on this album cover.

Lee Ann Womack, *Something Worth Leaving Behind* (MCA)—The something worth leaving behind was her old soccer mom image. A $100,000 photo shoot helmed by Matthew Rolston reveals a chic new Lee Ann.

Dixie Chicks, *Thank Heavens for Dale Evans* (Crystal Clear Sound)—Back when they performed on Dallas street corners (and before they got Natalie Maine as a lead singer), the Dale Evans worshipers released this 1992 album.

Dixie Chicks, *Wide Open Spaces* (Monument)—No fringed outfits here!

Shania Twain, *Shania Twain* (Mercury)—Hey, check out this chick from the Great White North singing "Dance with the One That Brought You." She's so wholesome!

Shania Twain, *The Woman in Me* (Mercury)—Don't mess with this sexy babe who demands to know "Whose Bed Have Your Boots Been Under?"

Faith Hill, *Cry* (Warner Bros.)—Cindy Crawford's shaking in her boots because this supermodel mom looks hotter than ever.

Chapter 12

Sharp-Dressed Men

Everyone knows what George Strait looks like: starched Western shirt, Wrangler jeans, Justin boots, Resistol hat. He looked like that when he made his MCA debut in 1981, and he's looked like that ever since. It's an image that has become the model for what a contemporary male country singer looks like: a cowboy.

That's why it's so disturbing to see him in the first few scenes of his 1992 movie, *Pure County*. George with a ponytail, beard, and sparkly jacket? It's so terribly wrong. "A George Strait or Alan Jackson, true artists like that are not about trying to look flashy," says fashion columnist Nicole Melton. "I just can't imagine they'd be worried about hair or clothes. I doubt they're perusing magazines for their next look. They don't have to worry about it, and I'm sure they don't."

In real life, George Strait dresses like a cowboy because he is authentically a cowboy. He runs his own roping invitational rodeo and is a proud card-carrying member of the Professional Rodeo Cowboys Association. And in case you're wondering, he still has a full head of hair under that hat.

The Hat Act

The word "Western" was dropped from "country & western," yet the Western look endures. "When I first got into country radio, I asked, 'What's up with the hats?'" Tonya Campos, assistant program director and music director for southern California's KZLA, says with a laugh. Alan Jackson even wore his cowboy hat water skiing in the "Chatahoochee" video. (Give Kenny Chesney credit that he didn't insist on wearing his snorkeling in the "How Forever Feels" video.)

There are several reasons why cowboy imagery is alive and kicking long after Roy Rogers and Gene Autry are dead. It's a very American look that appeals to the way Americans like to picture themselves. Think the Marlboro Man or President Reagan at home on the ranch. In addition, many of the acts wearing the hat actually sing about being cowboys (Tim McGraw's "The Cowboy in Me," Toby Keith's "Should've Been a Cowboy") or

the rodeo life (George Strait's "Amarillo by Morning," Garth Brooks's "Rodeo"). Don't overlook the fact that quite a few singers come from Texas or Oklahoma, where it's not unheard of to sport a Stetson.

But most important, a cowboy hat looks flattering on almost everybody. Yes, a lot of these guys only wear the cowboy hat when they're "on duty," but off duty, these same guys very rarely venture anywhere without some sort of head covering. Baseball caps, do-rags, and knit caps are worn even on the tour bus or in the recording studio. Given a choice, what would you rather see on stage, a guy in a do-rag or a Stetson?

Cowboys Wear Cowboy Shirts

"Brooks and Dunn come in and are so nice," declares Katy K, vintage cowboy shirt connoisseur and proprietress of Nashville's Katy K Designs. "They buy a whole bunch of stuff."

Stylist Renee Fowler concurs. "Brooks and Dunn are definitely icons who are true to who they are. They're classic cowboys."

Wish your boyfriend was more like Kix and Ronnie? For less than $100 you can transform him into a reasonable facsimile. It's easy as pie, because the Neon Rodeo and Wild West Show headliners have their own line of shirts made by Panhandle Slim, which retail for honest workingman prices.

Or you can go vintage shopping. Renee Fowler suggests, "That's my favorite way to shop for men's cowboy shirts. To establish a Brooks and Dunn look, search out Wrangler shirts at vintage shops. Try to find shirts from the sixties. They had a really good fit at that time. Great use of fabrics."

Katy K recommends the fifties' shirts, which are hard to come by but can occasionally be scored off eBay, though not at bargain prices. She adds that she's now selling a lot of the seventies' shirts. "The seventies' stuff is usually tighter, you know, that Urban Cowboy thing. It was cut slimmer, even the men's shirts have darts. The fabric tends to be cotton/poly. The embroidery has that kind of hippie thing going on. The fifties' shirts are rayon gabardine. More of a boxy cut. Better fabrics, and beautiful embroidery."

No More Rhinestone Cowboys

Nowadays everyone wants to be George Strait. In days of old, everyone wanted to be Hank Williams. And the man who made Hank Williams look like Hank Williams was legendary Western costume designer Nudie. Everyone knew you were a star if you wore a Nudie suit. Today, Manuel is the man to turn to for upscale stage outfits and award show threads.

"For male artists, it's a status symbol to be able to afford your first Manuel suit," explains journalist Beverly Keel, who profiled the designer for *People* magazine. "You want a gold record, a number-one hit, and a Manuel suit. His clothes are works of art. And priced accordingly."

Although Manuel is the former son-in-law of Nudie and is responsible for Gram Parson's famous marijuana leaf–embroidered white suit, his designs are not so easy to categorize.

"Remember, Manuel was the one who put Johnny Cash in black," Beverly Keel points out. "Manuel is a costumer as opposed to a fashion designer. And if you're thinking of those Porter Wagoner suits, you're way out of touch. Marty Stuart, who has probably over four hundred Manuel suits, still dresses

like that. But he's the only one. Manuel has evolved as fashions have evolved. He does Brooks and Dunn, Kenny Chesney, Keith Urban, and Brad Paisley. Manuel had more designs on the red carpet at the CMAs last year than ever."

Manuel works with an act to help them achieve their vision of themselves. His daughter Morelia says, "People come in and say they don't really know what they want, but somewhere in their heart, they know."

We also have Manuel to thank for Dwight Yoakam's tight, tight jeans. Morelia says with a laugh, "Lots and lots of patching. Dwight wears them out, my dad just patches and sews over, and they're good to go."

No Shoes, No Shirt, No Problems

Not everyone wears Manuel. Toby Keith loves to tell the story of his early touring days when he would follow Rhett Akins on stage. Rhett wore Manuel, Toby wore what he calls a wifebeater. It was the dead of summer and after a few shows even the dry cleaners wouldn't get within ten feet of Rhett's jacket.

Because touring season runs during the hottest part of the year, many guys go sleeveless. Kenny Chesney rips the arms off vintage concert T-shirts. To carry off the look, he spends a lot of time at the gym and takes his personal trainer on tour. Kenny's

casual look is highly appropriate for the guy who loves the island lifestyle. He sings about it, showcases it in his videos, and even totes a little bit with him all the time in the form of his trademark shell necklace. He also wears very, very tight jeans. And turns around a lot on stage, mostly while doing a silly dance thing, but it works for him. For award ceremonies, he wears Manuel (what else!).

Found in Every Cowboy's Closet

Garth Brooks also wears very, very tight jeans, but in his case it's a quick-fix solution for too many weak moments at Taco

Bell. Documented in his many TV specials, Garth's stage-look also includes outrageously striped Mo Betta shirts. But his publicist assures us that if you looked in Garth's closet lately you'd discover quite a few Wrangler shirts.

It there's any brand that defines country music, it would be Wrangler. When *Country Weekly* covered the concerts at Fan Fair 2002, the magazine included a photograph of female audience members holding up a homemade sign: "Show us your Wranglers."

"Wrangler jeans are never going anywhere," swears image consultant Renee Fowler. "They are definitely on our true blue cowboys. Alan Jackson and a lot of the more established icons are still wearing their Wranglers." Newer artists Brad Paisley, Blake Shelton, and Darryl Worley have modeled the jeans in Wrangler print ads.

"What could be more appealing than a handsome guy wearing jeans, boots, and a cowboy hat singing about the depth of his love for his lady?" sighs fan Leigh Ann Sanders. Millions of country-loving girls agree this is indeed the definition of a sharp-dressed man.

Various Artists, *Sharp Dressed Men: Tribute to ZZ Top* (RCA)— Always nicely dressed Brad Paisley gets the privilege of handling the title song in this collection of country covers.

George Strait, *Latest Greatest Straitest Hits* (MCA)—Still working the tried-and-true image.

Alan Jackson, *Drive* (Arista)—On the cover of his best album yet, Alan looks great in a simple flannel shirt.

Brooks & Dunn, *Steers and Stripes* (Arista)—F.Y.I., Panhandle Slim sells a shirt decorated with the steers and stripes motif.

Various Artists, *Return of the Grievous Angel/A Tribute to Gram Parsons* (Almo Records)—A 1999 benefit album executive produced by Emmylou Harris, featuring Gram's famous suit on the cover.

Dwight Yoakam, *Dwightlive* (Reprise)—It's not all about the tight jeans. The man puts on a killer show.

Kenny Chesney, *Greatest Hits* (BNA)—Forget about the hits, Kenny is pictured on the cover doing a male version of a wet T-shirt contest (emerging from water wearing his hat and white shirt). Yeehaw!

Chapter **13**

Sex and the Country

Poor Carrie, Miranda, Charlotte, and Samantha. Those *Sex and the City* girls have such a hard time when all they need to do is follow Eva Gabor's example and give up that Manhattan lifestyle for a little *Green Acres*. As country music videos illustrate, male/female relationships are much easier for those who have gone country.

Don't Settle for Less Than Tim McGraw and Paris

We know the ultimate romance is out there because we've seen it! One look at the "Let's Make Love" video (or, as we like to think of it, Tim and Faith's *Last Tango in Paris*) makes it perfectly clear why Faith Hill is always knocked up. Her hubby is sex personified.

Forget the Overalls, Wear Short Skirts

In "Man! I Feel Like a Woman!" Shania Twain advises the best outfit to wear is a guy's shirt and a short skirt. We know it works because Tim McGraw claims he's knocked out by a girl's mini skirt in the song "Something Like That."

The Easiest Way to Pick Up a Guy Is to Admire His Vehicle, Whatever It May Be

In the song "Pickup Man," Joe Diffie reveals his belief that owning a truck makes a man irresistible to women. In "Mercury Blues," Alan Jackson thinks it's his car that drives the girls crazy. But Kenny Chesney is the most delusional, proclaiming "She Thinks My Tractor's Sexy." Kenny's girl says the way the John Deere tills the dirt is a real turn-on. In the same song, the girl also compliments Kenny on his farmer's tan, but that's going a little too far!

⋆⁺* If You Want to Hook a Guy, ⋆⁺* Learn to Fish

In the video for "I'm Going to Miss Her (the Fishing Song)," Brad leaves his girlfriend to go fishing with the guys. The trick to keeping a guy like Brad, then, is to go fishing with him. (A girl being a bass fisher is also listed as a selling point in the Ricochet song "Daddy's Money.")

For girls willing to get up early to catch some bass, manly man Toby Keith reveals what guys know about fishing: Location is everything—pick a spot where brush piles up close to the bank. Don't even bother with lures—live bait is a must. Toby recommends putting a hook through a four-inch shad's tail. He swears this will work with catfish as well as bass. And if a girl is lucky, it will catch her a man as well!

To Dance or Not to Dance

This is a tricky one. Many country songs endorse dancing, but as a metaphor for life. When Lee Ann Womack says "I Hope You Dance," she doesn't mean you should drag a reluctant partner onto the floor. Many guys hate dancing, so this will not endear you to them. If the guy's up for a little "Boot Scootin' Boogie," then yes, dance. But don't force it or you could end up with the proverbial "Achy Breaky Heart."

Don't Panic If You Wake Up to Find Him Gone

If Gary Allan's "Man of Me" video is any indication, your guy has probably risen early to do some manly stuff like ride his motorcycle, skip stones in a pond, or play a little golf. Go ahead and get dressed in your sexiest outfit. He'll be back.

⋆ Get Rid of a *⋆*
No-Good Guy

No more standing by men who are abusive. If things get really bad, the girls in "Goodbye Earl" found that a little something deadly mixed in with the black-eyed peas will permanently solve the problem.

Faith Hill, *Breathe* (Warner Bros.)—You know Tim just loves her to death.

Joe Diffie, *16 Biggest Hits* (Epic)—How to pick up a "Pickup Man."

Alan Jackson, *A Lot About Livin' (and a Little 'Bout Love)* (Arista)—Check out the cover and see if you don't agree that Alan's motorcycle is pretty sexy too.

Kenny Chesney, *Everywhere We Go* (BNA)—Forget about Kenny's tractor, let's talk about those muscles! Has any man ever looked sexier in overalls?

Brad Paisley, *Part II* (Arista)—Maybe in Part III Brad will invite some girls to come along.

Lee Ann Womack, *I Hope You Dance* (MCA)—If we had a stunning Cinderella gown like the one Lee Ann wears on the cover of this CD, we'd dance way past midnight.

Gary Allan, *Alright Guy* (MCA)—As a romeo, Gary Allan is more than just all right.

Chapter 14

Girls Just Want to Have Fun

Back in Loretta Lynn's day, they called it honky-tonkin'. Going out to the local club to see a live band or play the jukebox. A little dancing, a little drinking, a little sex in a pickup truck parked out back.

In 1980 they made a movie about a Texas honky-tonk and started an *Urban Cowboy* craze. All of a sudden bars from Boston to Seattle imported bales of hay and hired line dance instructors. While the club boom has waned over the years, there are still a few watering holes where a girl can have a little *Coyote Ugly*—style fun. Let's hit Nashville's hotspots to discover what it takes to paint the town red, country style.

Bagging the Next Tim McGraw

Faith Hill hooked up with Tim McGraw on their 1996 Spontaneous Combustion tour, but she was late on the scene. Many a girl first laid eyes on Tim McGraw years before when he was gigging around Nashville's Printers Alley hoping to score a record deal. So don't be shy about going after that unknown hunk leading the club in a spirited version of "Down on the Farm." He really could turn out to be the next big thing.

Getting Wild at the Wildhorse

"Country tunes are terrific for dancing, be it two-step, swing, line dancing, or cheek-to-cheek slow dancing," enthuses fan Leigh Ann Sanders.

"Couples dancing is always big," says Chris Lucas, DJ and dance instructor at Nashville's famous Wildhorse Saloon, where a 3,300-square-foot dance floor is large enough to accommodate eight hundred line dancers. "We'll see some good swingers in here occasionally. But if you go to Texas, it's a whole different world—all two-stepping."

Don't worry if you don't know the steps. Chris counsels, "Country bars are not just about country dancing! A lot of your country bars will play eighties music, and your country stars will play rock-and-roll stuff. When it comes down to it, it's all just about having fun."

Chris complains that "a lot of the recent country stuff you can't dance to," but he can always count on Shania's "Man! I Feel Like a Woman!" to get people onto the floor.

So how's a girl supposed to move her feet when she wants to feel like a woman? "You can do the electric slide to any song there is," Chris suggests. "That's why everyone likes it. It's easy, everyone knows it, and everyone from little eleven-year-olds all the way to ninety-year-olds can do it."

Chris rattles off the steps:

- ❀ Grapevine to the right

- ❀ Grapevine to the left

- ❀ Three steps back

- ❀ Step, stomp

- ❀ Step, stomp

- ❀ Quarter-turn to your left

"That's how easy that dance is!"

171

Eight Seconds You'll Never Forget

Gilley's, the famous *Urban Cowboy* honky-tonk, may have burned to the ground in 1989, but the mechanical bull that gave Debra Winger such a thrill is back! Not in Nashville, but in cities across the nation, bars are doing great business with weekly bull riding contests. "I put a girl on it the other night who had never ridden before," says Thomas Blankenship, who runs the bull at a Hollywood club. "She actually won the contest—level six! She did awesome. Totally blew everybody away!"

For girls aspiring to be indoor rodeo queens, Thomas gives the following tips for riding the bull:

- Keep your pelvis up against the horn of the bull. (The horn is where the handle is.)

- Lean back.

- If you're right-handed, hold on with your left hand, keep your other arm up to keep your balance.

- Lean back as far as you can.

- Roll your hips when the bull is kicking.

- Keep your feet in front.

- Squeeze with your legs and your knees.

Thomas explains, "The reason why you roll your hips and lean back is you're counteracting the bull. When the bull bucks, you got to lean back otherwise you'll fly out frontward. Remember, it's pretty much all about balance and timing. You'll get the hang of it."

Sing Along with José Cuervo

Drinking songs (and drinking) have always been a staple of country music. You can't beat Garth Brooks's "Friends in Low Places" as the ultimate bar tune, but there are several other modern drinking song favorites that a girl can put on the jukebox to get everyone singing along:

❀ **"Ten Rounds with Jose Cuervo"**—Tracy Byrd illustrates how even the worst night in a bar gets better as the rounds keep coming.

❀ **"Ten Feet Tall & Bulletproof"**—Travis Tritt describes how one feels after downing a few.

❀ **"Two Piña Coladas"**—Garth Brooks realizes if he's got two hands he can easily handle two glasses.

❀ **"Margaritaville"**—Alan Jackson joins Jimmy Buffet searching for that infamous elusive salt shaker.

❀ **"Pour Me"**—Finally, a lively modern girl's drinking song, courtesy of Trick Pony's Heidi Newfield.

Got Milk?

In Kenny Chesney's "The Good Stuff," a kindly bartender reminds a lost soul of what's really important in life, then pours him a glass of milk. That might be okay for Kenny, but girls prefer bartenders who recommend Sex on the Beach.

Carly Lanin tends the bar at Tootsie's Orchid Lounge. A Nashville fixture since 1960, the Orchid Lounge was originally run by Hattie Louise Tatum Bess (nicknamed Tootsie) and was a popular hangout for songwriters such as Kris Kristofferson and Willie Nelson. Patsy Cline's husband used to warm the barstools while his wife performed across the alley at the Grand Ole Opry, then joined him for a cold one afterward. In more recent years, Terri Clark performed on the bar's tiny stage before she got her record deal, and countless music videos have been shot there.

For those ready to become full-fledged members of the Honky-Tonk Bar Association, we've cribbed together some drink recipes (each makes one drink) based on bartender Carly's recommendations.

Sex on the Beach

grapefruit juice

cranberry juice

1 oz. vodka

3/4 oz. peach schnapps

Fill a highball glass halfway with the fruit juices, then stir in the alcohol.

Buttery Nipple

1/2 oz. butterscotch schnapps

1/2 oz. Irish cream

To make this layered shot, fill a shot glass halfway with butterscotch schnapps. Layer in the Irish cream with a spoon so it floats on top.

Rocky Mountain
M*therf*cker

½ oz. amaretto

½ oz. Yukon Jack

2 splashes Rose's Lime Juice

Mix in a shaker over ice. Strain into a shot glass.

Lemon Drop

1 lemon wedge

1 tsp. white sugar

1 shot Absolut Citron

Dip the lemon wedge in sugar. Do the shot, then immediately bite/suck the sweetened lemon.

Alabama Slammer

1 oz. Southern Comfort

1 oz. amaretto

1/2 oz. sloe gin

1 splash lemon juice

Into a highball glass, pour the Southern Comfort, amaretto, and gin. Stir. Add the lemon juice.

Redheaded Slut

1 1/2 oz. peach schnapps

1 1/2 oz. Jagermeister

3 oz. cranberry juice

Mix and shake with ice. Strain into shot glasses.

Mind Eraser

2 oz. vodka

2 oz. Kahlua

2 oz. club soda

In an ice-filled whisky sour glass, layer in vodka, then Kahlua. Top with club soda. Do not stir. Insert a straw and drink quickly.

Absolut Stress

1 oz. Absolut Vodka

1 oz. Malibu rum

1/2 oz. peach schnapps

1 oz. cranberry juice

1 oz. orange juice

1 oz. pineapple juice

Mix in a shaker with ice. Strain into a collins glass.

Carly also recommends the old standbys: margaritas, tequila, Jack Daniel's, and Budweiser.

Pony up to the bar, girls, drinks are on us!

Various Artists, *Urban Cowboy Soundtrack* (Elektra/Asylum)—Yes, it's dated, but it's still a whole lot of fun.

Various Artists, *Cowboy Ugly Soundtrack* (Curb)—Better than the movie, that's for sure.

Tim McGraw, *Tim McGraw* (Curb)—The very first song on Tim's very first album is "Welcome to the Club."

Terri Clark, *How I Feel* (Mercury)—Tootsie's cowboy hat–wearing chanteuse sings about guys who are easy on the eyes.

Garth Brooks, *The Hits* (Capitol)—"Friends in Low Places," indeed!

Tracy Byrd, *Ten Rounds* (RCA)—While it's hard to top his classic "Lifestyles of the Not So Rich and Famous," the "Jose Cuervo" tune comes close. P.S.: How unfair is it that Mr. Byrd has eyelashes girls would die for.

Trick Pony, *Trick Pony* (Warner Bros.)—Leave it to Heidi and the boys to rhyme "Okie" with "karaoake."

Chapter **15**

Happy Trails
to You

Who wouldn't want to be Donna Fargo? She's the singer/
songwriter who looked around at her life and realized
she was "The Happiest Girl in the Whole U.S.A."

Certainly there are times when a girl feels like she could wrestle the title away from Ms. Fargo. On those particular days, one can find oneself happily chirping along to SHeDAISY ditties.

But even cowgirls get the blues. That's when a girl realizes there's nothing better than a sad country song to induce a cathartic cry. Time to put the late, great Keith Whitley in heavy rotation.

By now you've undoubtedly discovered country music's ultimate appeal: No matter what emotion a girl is feeling or what situation she is facing, she can find the appropriate soundtrack to her life in a country song.

The vast catalog has the depth and breadth to cater to your every need. "People sometimes criticize country music for having too many songs about heartache," remarks fan Hillary Warren, "yet no one can deny that heartache is a reality for everyone. Country music reminds people that they definitely aren't alone in whatever they feel."

"Country music resonates with so many truths about life," adds fan Leigh Ann Sanders, "such as finding love, losing love, and the joys and pains of simple everyday existence. The songs truly address what is important in life and speak directly to your soul."

Although no one knows what the future will bring (for us or for country music, for that matter), we're willing to bet a girl will always be able to find comfort and joy in a country song.

On behalf of all the girls who contributed to this guide, we wish you all the best as you put together the soundtrack to your life.

Happy trails to you!

SHeDAISY, *Knock on the Sky* (Lyric Street)—Play this when you're feeling so happy you want to kiss the sky.

Keith Whitley, *Wherever You Are Tonight* (BNA)—No matter how rough life gets, you'll feel better after listening to this posthumous release of songs from Keith's private vault. (Whitley's *Don't Close Your Eyes* is another good bet. In fact, it's one of three records Tim McGraw would take with him to a desert island.)

k.d. lang, *Even Cowgirls Get the Blues: Music from the Motion Picture* (Warner Bros.)—The perfect soundtrack for a blue mood. If you're looking for a more cheery soundtrack, try *Hope Floats.*

Various Artists, *Country Heartaches* (Hip-O Records)—In parting, we leave you with this thought: Girls who have gone country know how to survive heartache.

Various Artists, *Country Lovin': Songs from the Heart* (Rhino Records)—Girls who have gone country know how to love.

Various Artists, *Ultimate Country Party* (Arista)—Girls who have gone country know how to party.

Various Artists, *Superstar Country Dance Hits* (Curb)—And girls who have gone country know how to dance.

So, girls, what are you waiting for? Load up your CD player and go country!

Notes

Introduction

1   **"What do you get"**: Most recently told by Noah Edelson.

1   **on 21 percent of U.S. stations**: Radio station statistics by M Street Format Monitor, April 2001, cited in Country Music Association, *2001 CMA Country Music Industry Overview,* www.cmaworld.com, August 6, 2002, p. 3.

2   **on a televised concert special**: *All Access: Toby Keith,* A CMT Original Production, 2001.

2   **official promotional material**: *Play It Loud Enhanced CD,* Capitol Records, 2001.

2   **women buy the majority**: Fifty-four percent of all country music buyers are women, according to Country Music Association, *2001 CMA Country Music Industry Overview,* p. 3.

2   **CMT has a higher audience**: "Get in Step with the Times," *Time Warner Cable, Albany, New York Advertising Info,* 2002. According to Nielsen Media Research 3Q 2000, CMT ranked number one with Women 18–34 and Women 18–49 audience concentration.

2   **country radio stations identify their target**: Steve Carney, "Country Radio Is Now 'Music of the Suburbs,' " *Los Angeles Times,* March 8, 2002.

3 **best-selling country album of all time**: According to RIAA's platinum certifications.

3 **first two Dixie Chicks albums**: As of 2002, RIAA tallies *Wide Open Spaces* at 11 million and *Fly* at 10 million.

4 **"Martina's music"**: E-mail correspondence with Liz Beavers, September 6, 2002.

Chapter 1: Welcome to the Country Club

15 **"Country music is for everyone"**: Telephone conversation with Pam Tillis, September 27, 2002.

16 **Jodie has had her photo**: See the photos online at www.geocities.com/jodie3242.

17 **we asked Jodie to share**: Telephone conversation with Jodie Weckman, November 24, 2002.

17 **"Martina tries"**: E-mail correspondence with Liz Beavers, September 6, 2002.

Chapter 2: Seven Essential Hunks

23 **"With George Strait"**: Personal interview with Beverly Keel, August 20, 2002.

25 **Garth credits high energy cowboy singer**: *Inside Fame: Chris LeDoux*, A CMT Original Production, 2002.

25 **savvy Reba watched the audiences**: *The Garth Brooks Story*, an original radio special produced by Westwood One Entertainment, original airdate July 4, 1996.

33 **he confesses to be channeling**: Randy Lewis, "He Has a Way with the Ladies," *Los Angeles Times*, May 28, 2002.

36 **"are usually surprised at the older songs"**: E-mail correspondence with Kay Johnson, September 18, 2002.

39 **"fluff"**: Gary Allan *Alright Guy* press bio, prepared by MCA Nashville Publicity, August 2001.

39 **"starving for something"**: ibid.

39 **"Buck and Hag"**: ibid.

Chapter 3: Girls with Guitars and Guy Trouble

46 **Porter told Dolly**: *Showcase: Dolly Parton*, A CMT Original Production, 2001.

47 **"But until a dozen"**: Personal interview with Beverly Keel, August 20, 2002.

Chapter 4: The Hottest Trend Going

53 **Dan's wife**: *Bluegrass Special,* A CMT Original Production, 2002.

53 **buying more copies**: *SoundScan's Year-End Music Industry Report* identified the *O Brother, Where Art Thou?* soundtrack as the Top Country Album for 2001 with 3.5 million sales, with Garth Brooks's *Scarecrow* coming in second with 2.3 million.

54 **"Bluegrass gives the musicians"**: E-mail correspondence with Kori Frazier, October 1, 2002.

56 **violinist Sara Watkins:** All Nickel Creek information is from the official band *This Side* CD press bio, www.nickelcreek.com.

57 **"My father loved"**: Patty Loveless *Classics* press bio, Epic Records publicity, 1999.

57 **Invited to play a Ralph Stanley bluegrass festival**: Patty Loveless *Mountain Soul* press bio, 2002.

58 **Alison even goes so far**: *The Women of Country,* High Five Productions, 1993.

58 **"I had to get"**: Alana Nash, "Splendor in the Bluegrass," *Entertainment Weekly,* 2002.

Chapter 5: Treasure Hunting at the Hall of Fame

61 **"We've had many people who've worked here"**: All quotes from Diana Johnson are from a personal interview at the Country Music Hall of Fame and Museum, August 19, 2002.

67 **Dolly Parton shot back**: Dolly Parton, *Dolly: My Life and Other Unfinished Business* (New York: HarperCollins, 1994), p. 188.

68 **"If country had its own money"**: Telephone conversation with Bear Fisher, July 24, 2002.

Chapter 6: Record Shopping with Pam Tillis

74 **"do our hearts a lot of good"**: All quotes from Pam Tillis are from a telephone interview, September 27, 2002.

Chapter 7: The Loretta Lynn School of Success

81 **When Loretta Lynn agreed:** Country Music Association, *2001 CMA Country Music Industry Overview*, p. 4.

81 **Johnny Cash, when inducting:** Country Music Hall of Fame and Museum website page on inductee Loretta Lynn.

82 **Loretta admitted on CMT's:** *Inside Fame: Loretta Lynn*, A CMT Original Production, 2002.

83 **Garth Brooks remembers:** *Hunks with Hats*, Best Film & Video, 1990.

84 **"three chords and the truth":** Quote painted on the wall of the Country Music Hall of Fame and Museum, Nashville, Tennessee.

87 **"a bunch of songs":** Randy Lewis, "He Has a Way with the Ladies," *Los Angeles Times*, May 28, 2002.

90 **Clint Black claims:** *Hunks with Hats*, Best Film & Video, 1990.

90 **$25 million:** Country Music Association, *2001 CMA Country Music Industry Overview*, p. 3.

91 **telling her twins apart:** Lynn, Loretta with George Vecsey, *Coal Miner's Daughter* (New York: Warner Books, 1976), p. 162.

Chapter 8: Building the Perfect Country Star

96 **Toby Keith says:** *American Country Video, Part I*, 1994.

97 **Lee Ann Womack says:** Lee Ann Womack interviewed backstage at the Grand Old Opry, by CMT's Katie Cook, September 7, 2002.

97 **Loretta Lynn says:** Loretta Lynn interviewed by Charlie Rose, *The Charlie Rose Show*, 2002.

Chapter 9: Truly Outstanding Hair

111 **cast as LeAnn Rimes's grandmother:** Neil Pond, "She'll Never Be 'King of the Road,' But She's Already 'Queen of the Row,'" Country America.com.

112 **"that doesn't exist in nature":** Tim Ryan, "Here Come the Judds," *Honolulu Star-Bulletin*, July 6, 2000.

113 **Jo Dee names fellow carrottops:** Lou Carlozo, "Feel the Burn," On Tour with Shure.com, Shure Incorporated, summer 2001.

115 **"my life began":** "Star Stats: Faith Hill," *Country Weekly Online*, October 4, 2000.

117 **Robison said it was a by-product:** Mary Murphy, "Hearts of Dixie," *TV Guide*, April 22, 2000.

117 **Aretha Franklin**: SHeDAISY *Knock on the Sky* press bio, Lyric Street Records, 2002.

118 **"I think if I've"**: Emmylou Harris *Red Dirt Girl* press bio, Vector Management.

119 **"I think I got"**: ibid.

Chapter 10: Mullets and More

124 **he told record executives**: *Billy Ray Cyrus: The Video Collection,* Universal Music, 1993.

127 **years of chaotic living**: George Jones *The Rock: Stone Cold Country 2001* press bio, BNA/Bandit, 2001.

127 **"shock of untamed hair"**: Lyle Lovett *Anthology Vol. 1 Cowboy Man* press bio, Curb/MCA Nashville, September 2001.

128 **"girl vine"**: E. Jean Carroll, "Loving Lyle," *Esquire,* May 1994.

129 **Natalie Maines was thrilled**: "Marty Stuart News," Marty Stuart Fan Page, www.pagedepot.com/martystuart, September 9, 2002.

129 **"Marty Stuart always looks"**: Personal interview with Morelia, August 20, 2002.

131 **Travis Tritt can tell you**: *Inside Fame: Travis Tritt,* A CMT Original Production, 2002.

131 **Gary Morris–type**: Robert K. Oermann, liner notes from the album *Travis Tritt: The Rockin' Side,* Rhino Records.

131 **Travis realized**: *Inside Fame: Travis Tritt,* A CMT Original Production, 2002.

133 **what kind of shampoo**: Garth Brooks interviewed by Victoria Shaw on www.victoriashaw.com.

134 **"hair activist"**: *Inside Fame: Travis Tritt,* A CMT Original Production, 2002.

Chapter 11: Dixie Chic

137 **"Gone are the days"**: All quotes from Nicole Melton are from a telephone interview with Nicole Melton, August 20, 2002.

138 **Eddie Montgomery stumbled**: *Greatest 40 Outlaw Videos,* A CMT Original Production, 2002.

138 **Shania herself has no clue**: *Inside Fame: Shania Twain,* A CMT Original Production, 2002.

138 **"Before, Faith Hill"**: Personal interview with Beverly Keel, August 20, 2002.

139 **"When they first signed"**: All quotes from Renee Fowler are from a telephone interview with Renee Fowler, August 19, 2002.

140 **"You all can't say"**: Dennis Hunt, Edna Gundersen, Bruce Haring, and Steve Jones, "Wild Style Is Night's Key Note," *USA Today*, February 5, 1999.

140 **"You know, I caught"**: All quotes from Renee Fowler are from a telephone interview with Renee Fowler, August 19, 2002.

140 **Shania Twain was asked**: Hunt et al., "Wild Style Is Night's Key Note," *USA Today*, February 5, 1999.

141 **"Once an artist"**: All quotes from Renee Fowler are from a telephone interview with Renee Fowler, August 19, 2002.

143 **"The most important"**: ibid.

144 **"I think everybody"**: ibid.

145 **"Instead of Anna Sui"**: ibid.

145 **"At a store like bebe"**: Telephone interview with Nicole Melton, August 19, 2002.

Chapter 12: Sharp-Dressed Men

149 **"A George Strait"**: Telephone interview with Nicole Melton, August 19, 2002.

150 **"When I first got into country radio"**: Personal interview with Tonya Campos, July 2002.

151 **"Brooks and Dunn come in"**: Personal interview with Katy K, August 19, 2002.

152 **"Brooks and Dunn are definitely"**: Telephone interview with Renee Fowler, August 19, 2002.

153 **"That's my favorite way"**: ibid.

153 **"The seventies' stuff"**: Personal interview with Katy K, August 19, 2002.

153 **"For male artists, it's a status"**: Personal interview with Beverly Keel, August 20, 2002.

154 **"Remember, Manuel"**: ibid.

155 **"People come in"**: Personal interview with Morelia, August 20, 2002.

155 **"Lots and lots"**: ibid.

155 **Toby Keith loves to tell**: *Inside Fame: Toby Keith*, A CMT Original Production, 2002.

157 **his publicist**: Telephone conversation with Karen Byrd, August 19, 2002.

157　**"Show us your Wranglers"**: Neil Pond, "Welcome to Fan Fair," *Country Weekly*, July 23, 2002, p. 17.

157　**"Wrangler jeans are never"**: Telephone interview with Renee Fowler, August 19, 2002.

158　**"What could be more appealing"**: E-mail correspondence with Leigh Ann Sanders, October 2, 2002.

Chapter 13: Sex and the Country

164　**manly man Toby Keith reveals**: "The Cowboy Way," *TV Guide*, November 3, 2001.

Chapter 14: Girls Just Want to Have Fun

170　**"Country tunes are terrific"**: E-mail correspondence with Leigh Ann Sanders, October 2, 2002.

170　**"Couples dancing is always big"**: All quotes from Chris Lucas are from a personal interview at the Wildhorse, August 21, 2002.

172　**"I put a girl"**: All quotes from Thomas Blankenship are from a personal interview at the Saddle Ranch Chop House, September 2002.

175　**Carly's recommendations**: Personal interview with Carly Lanin at Tootsie's Orchid Lounge in Nashville, August 18, 2002.

Chapter 15: Happy Trails to You

184　**"People sometimes criticize"**: E-mail correspondence from Hillary Warren, October 1, 2002.

184　**"Country music resonates"**: E-mail correspondence from Leigh Ann Sanders, October 2, 2002.

185　**Tim McGraw would take**: "Name Your Three Desert Island CDs," Tim McGraw Facts 2002, www.timmcgraw.com.

Photo and Illustration Credits

12   Phil Vassar and daughter on the set of "American Child" video shoot. Courtesy of Arista Nashville, RCA Label Group, BMG.

16   Ira Dean, Heidi Newfield, fan Jodie Weckman, and Keith Burns at the Trick Pony meet-and-greet at Medina. Courtesy of Jodie Weckman, www.geocities.com/jodie3242.

20   George Strait as Dusty, Isabel Glasser as Harley in *Pure Country* publicity still, copyright 1992 Warner Bros. Photographer: Ron Phillips.

22   George Strait as Dusty in *Pure Country* publicity still, copyright 1992 Warner Bros. Photographer: Ron Phillips.

24   Garth Brooks performs the song "Beer Run" with his idol George Jones at the Thirty-fifth Annual Country Music Association Awards, broadcast from the Grand Ole Opry House in Nashville, November 7, 2001. Photographer: Tami Chappell/Reuters/TimePix.

27   Alan Jackson photographed against his Harley-Davidson motorcycle on his Brentwood, Tennessee, farm on March 9, 1992. Photographer: Acey Harper, Timepix.

30   Tim McGraw publicity photo. Courtesy of Jessie Schmidt, Schmidt Relations. Photographer: Steve Klein

32   Kenny Chesney performing at Mankato. Photographer: Jodie Weckman, www.geocities.com/jodie3242.

35   Toby Keith at the Mall of America for the *Unleashed* signing. Photographer: Jodie Weckman, www.geocities.com/jodie3242.

38   Gary Allan publicity photo for *Alright Guy*. Courtesy of MCA Nashville Publicity. Photographer: Tony Baker.

42   Deana Carter/*Everything's Gonna Be Alright* album cover, Capitol Records, copyright 1998.

46   Dolly Parton publicity photo. Courtesy of Sugar Hill Records Media. Photographer: Annie Leibovitz.

52   Alison Krauss + Union Station/*New Favorite* album cover, Rounder Records Corp., copyright 2001.

55   Nickel Creek publicity photo. Courtesy of Sugar Hill Records Media. Photographer: John Chaisson.

58   Dolly Parton greets fans during an appearance on NBC television's *Today Show* in New York on July 5, 2002. Photographer: Peter Morgan, Timepix.

60   Trisha Yearwood publicity photo. Courtesy of Force Management. Photographer: Russ Harrington.

68   Country Music Hall of Fame and Museum, Nashville, Tennessee. Photographer: Kim Adelman.

72 Pam Tillis publicity photo. Courtesy of the baker/northrop media group. Photographer: Russ Harrington.

76 Record albums. Photographer: Kim Adelman.

80 Sissy Spacek as Loretta Lynn, with Minnie Pearl and Ernest Tubb in a publicity still from the motion picture *Coal Miner's Daughter,* copyright 1980 Universal City Studios, Inc.

82 Loretta Lynn publicity photo. Courtesy of Hot Schatz Public Relations. Photographer: Peter Nash.

85 Sissy Spacek as Loretta Lynn, Tommy Lee Jones as husband Mooney (Doo) Lynn, publicity still from the motion picture *Coal Miner's Daughter,* copyright 1980 Universal City Studios, Inc.

89 Sissy Spacek as Loretta Lynn, Beverly D'Angelo as Patsy Cline, publicity still from the motion picture *Coal Miner's Daughter,* copyright 1979 Universal City Studios, Inc.

90 Sissy Spacek as Loretta Lynn, Jennifer and Jessica Beasley as twin daughters Patsy and Peggy Lynn, publicity still from the motion picture *Coal Miner's Daughter,* copyright 1979 Universal City Studios, Inc.

94 Tim McGraw publicity photo. Courtesy of Jessie Schmidt, Schmidt Relations.

99 Eddie Montgomery and Troy Gentry of Montgomery Gentry. Courtesy of Sony Music Entertainment, Inc., and Darlene Bieber of Schmidt Relations. Photographer: Marina Chavez.

104 *The Girls' Guide to Country* Tammy Award. Photographer: Kim Adelman.

107 Crystal Gayle publicity photo. Courtesy of Crystal Gayle.

109 Dolly Parton publicity photo. Courtesy of Sugar Hill Records Media. Photographer: Annie Leibowitz.

110 *Reba McEntire's Greatest Hits* CD cover, MCA, copyright 1992.

111 *Reba McEntire Greatest Hits, Volume III—I'm a Survivor* CD cover, MCA Nashville, copyright 2001.

112 Naomi and Wynonna Judd at Big K. Photographer: Jodie Weckman, www.geocities.com/jodie3242.

113 Jo Dee Messina/*Burn* CD cover, Curb Records, Inc. copyright 2000.

114 Faith Hill arrives at the Twenty-seventh Annual People's Choice Awards in Pasadena, California, January 7, 2001. Photographer: Rose Prouser/Reuters/Timepix.

116 Dixie Chicks publicity photo. Courtesy of Kathy Allmand, Front Page Publicity.

117 SHeDAISY publicity photo. Courtesy of LGB Media.

118 Emmylou Harris publicity photo. Courtesy of Vector Management. Photographer: Michael Wilson.

122   Billy Ray Cyrus in concert. Photographer: Paul Natkin/Photo Reserve.

125   Willie Nelson publicity photo. Courtesy of Lost Highway. Photographer: Mark Seliger.

126   George Jones publicity photo. Courtesy of Bandit Records. Photographer: Jim Shea.

128   Lyle Lovett publicity photo. Courtesy of Vector Management. Photographer: Michael Wilson.

129   Marty Stuart outside Manuel. Courtesy of Morelia/Manuel. Photographer: Chuck Jones.

131   Travis Tritt publicity photo. Courtesy of Kathy Allmand, Front Page Publicity. Photographer: Ronald C. Modra.

132   Alan Jackson publicity photo. Courtesy of Force Management. Photographer: Tony Phipps.

133   Garth Brooks accepts the Award of Merit at the Twenty-ninth annual American Music Awards in Los Angeles, January 9, 2002. Photographer: Mike Blake, Reuters News Service.

136   Shania Twain at the Country Music Association Awards on October 4, 2000. Photographer: Tami Chappell/Reuters/Timepix.

139ff. All original costume illustrations by Kevin Ackerman.

148   George Strait as Dusty in *Pure Country* publicity still, copyright 1992 Warner Bros. Photographer: Ron Phillips.

152ff. All original costume illustrations by Kevin Ackerman.

160   Faith Hill and Tim McGraw performing during Jamboree in the Hills, Morriston, Ohio, July 16, 1998. Photographer: Laura Farr/Timepix.

163   Questionably sexy tractor. Photographer: Kim Adelman.

164   Brad Paisley on the set of "I'm Going to Miss Her (the Fishing Song)" video shoot. Courtesy of Arista Nashville, RCA Label Group, BMG.

168   The Dixie Chicks smoking cigars at the pool table at the Sony bash after their win at the Thirty-second Annual Country Music Association Awards, Nashville, Tennessee, September 23, 1998. Photographer: Tammie Arroyo/Timepix.

173   Bar patron Bear Fisher on the mechanical bull. Photographer: Kim Adelman.

175   Tootsie's Orchid Lounge in Nashville, Tennessee. Photographer: Kim Adelman.

182   SHeDAISY publicity photo. Courtesy of LGB Media.

186   Toby Keith and fan Bonnie Henry at a meet-and-greet. Courtesy of Bonnie Henry.

Acknowledgments

The author wishes to thank (in alphabetical order):

Sylvia Abumuhor

Kevin Ackerman

Molly-Dodd Wheeler Adams

Craig Adelman

Howard Adelman

Nancy Adelman

Kathy Allmand

Cary Baker

Barbara Barthelmes

Darlene Bieber

David Birdsell

Thomas Blankenship

Allen Brown

Maria Burton

Tonya Campos

Matt Cartsonis

Susan Cartsonis

William Clark

Becky Cole

Caroline Cunningham

Beth Datlowe

Emily Deaderick

Maria de la Torre

Leslie Dinaberg

Noah Edelson

Debbie Felton

Lance Finley

Bear Fisher

Kim Fowler

Renee Fowler

Kathleen French

Crystal Gayle

Natalie Gildea

Holly Gleason

Linda Gordon

Cynthia Grimson

Marcia Groff

Schatzi Hageman

Bryan Hale

Andrea Harling

Cindy Hazen

Carol Heikkinen

Bonnie Henry

Petra Hoy

Doug "Disco" Hylton

Andre Jacquemetton

Maria Jacquemetton

Deb Jarnes

Diana Johnson

Kay Johnson

Sara Juarez

Amy Jurist

`Katy K

Beverly Keel

Deborah Keith

David King

Zak Klobucher

Carly Lannin

Joel Leslie

Chris Lucas

John Lytle

Holly Mandel

Manuel

Carol May

Clare McMahon

Nicole Melton

Andrew Mersmann

Loren Miller

Dean Minerd

Maura Mooney

Morelia

Paul Natkin

Louise Neibold

Kimberly Nordling-Curtin

Lynn Padilla

Leslie Paulin

Jeff Payne

Bob Pederson

Laura Phillips

Catherine Pollock

Matt Pugh

Doris Quon

Douglas Ross

Ralph Sall

Leigh Ann Sanders

Jessie Schmidt

Mara Schwartz

Kimberly Sharp

Carol Sheridan

Katie Shiban

Tricia Stewart Shiu

Lesley Marlene Siegel

Hazel Smith

William Smithson

Donnie Snow

Cathy Tanzer

Pam Tillis

Rona Tuccillo

Peggy Van Norman

Angie Waack

Alana Watkins

Jodie Weckman

Craig Wells

Michael Wiese

Wendy Wilson

Alison Winward

Index

About the Author

Kim Adelman is the founder of GirlsGuidetoCountry.com.
She is also the author of *The Girls' Guide to Elvis.*